P R O F E S S I O N A L
HEADSHOTS

PROFESSIONAL HEADSHOTS

HOW TO MAKE MONEY SHOOTING PORTFOLIOS FOR ACTORS

john hart

AMPHOTO
AN IMPRINT OF WATSON-GUPTILL PUBLICATIONS
NEW YORK

COURTESY OF HERB FOGELSON

John Hart is a professional photographer and playwright who lives and works in New York City. For him, photographing new talent is a rewarding, enriching experience. Hart is also the author of two other Amphoto titles, *50 Portrait Lighting Techniques for Pictures That Sell* (1983) and *Lighting for Action* (1992).

Model credits:
Title page: Lela Spencer, Michael Sayer
Contents page: Michael Lucci

Editorial concept by Robin Simmen
Edited by Liz Harvey
Designed by Jay Anning
Graphic production by Hector Campbell

Copyright © 1994 by John Hart
First published in 1994 in New York by Amphoto,
an imprint of Watson-Guptill Publications,
a division of BPI Communications, Inc.,
1515 Broadway, New York, NY 10036

Printed in the United States of America

Library of Congress Cataloging-in-Publication Data

Hart, John (John Patrick).
    Professional headshots: how to make money shooting portfolios for actors / by John Hart.
    Includes index.
    ISBN 0-8174-5606-6 (pbk.)
    1. Portrait photography.   2. Actors—Portraits.   I. Title.
    TR575.H264   1994   94-15148
    778.9'2—dc20   CIP

2 3 4 5 6 7 8 9 / 02 01 00 99 98 97 96

*To my sister, Catherine Hart, for being,
once again, my confidante during the making of this book.*

———————————

My thanks to Liz Harvey, my astute editor; Robin Simmen, who initiated the concept; Joe Beninati Labs, for the great black-and-white prints for this book; specifically, Phillip for processing, Andy for printing, and Ron, "Mr. In Charge"; Jim McKenney, the word-processing whiz at Carnegie Press; Ron Massaro at Summer Productions; and, finally, all the actors, actresses, managers, and talent agents who were kind enough to participate in the production of this book.

CONTENTS

INTRODUCTION

In order for actors to get professional work in the theater, on television, or in films, they must be represented by a professional headshot. This is true of every part of the broad spectrum that comprises the show-business industry. No matter where in the world actors work, whether in New York, Hollywood, Chicago, Dallas, Orlando, England, France, Italy, Russia, Japan, or Brazil, they must have a 8 x 10 black-and-white, professionally photographed headshot. This picture is sometimes referred to as a "glossy," although the reproduction of the original image is most often printed on matte paper. Naturally, the more professional a headshot looks and the more professionally photographed it is, the greater the chance that it will enable an actor to get work.

Jeff Knapp's legit headshot is a perfect example of a photograph that satisfies an actor's need for a

professional shot that will leave a favorable impression in casting offices. Everything about his headshot suggests that he is about to make it big. This striking picture makes the best of Jeff's good looks, particularly his intense eyes. His eye contact is strong, and he projects the quiet self-confidence that spells professional. His pose makes him appear to be quite relaxed. His medium-length hair doesn't interfere with or dominate his direct gaze toward the lens. I selected medium-tan makeup for a natural look.

I had Jeff wear a black T-shirt and chose a soft, mottled background so viewers will concentrate on him. I placed the key light to his right in order to accentuate his bone structure, bounced the reflector into the resulting shaded area on his left side to keep it from going black, and used minimal hairlighting.

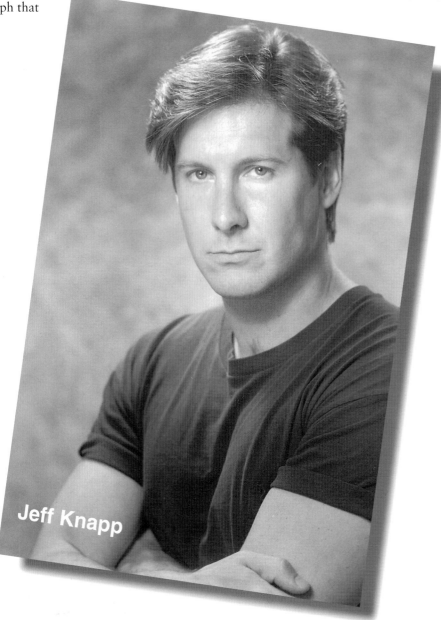

Jeff Knapp

THE IMPORTANCE OF A GREAT HEADSHOT

For beginning actors and performers, having a high-quality headshot made by a professional headshot photographer is an absolute must. This photograph is, in essence, their calling card and, hence, their door-opener into the working world of entertainment. Once the headshot is mailed out to the agents, managers, and casting people who are responsible for getting actors a role or part in a play, film, or soap opera, the headshot will, if it is good, help tremendously to "sell" the talent. A great black-and-white 8 x 10 spells success when an actor has the talent to back it up. However, if the headshot is badly done—for example, if it is poorly illuminated or fails to project the performer's personality—it can kill an actor's chances of getting started in the entertainment industry and leaves the performer waiting for the telephone to ring; it also screams "amateur."

Keep in mind that thousands of headshots cross the desks of managers, talent agents, and casting people everyday. The top-notch shots stand out, are noticed, compete, and win out over all the others. Great headshots are much more likely than weak headshots to prompt a casting person to call the agents who, in turn, will call the talent in to audition for a specific acting job. Headshots that don't suggest or reveal anything interesting about the talent will wind up in the wastepaper basket.

I must make an important point here. Once the agent or casting people respond to an exceptional headshot, they expect the person who subsequently walks into their office to look like the person in the picture. The headshot should be an accurate representation of the individual talent. Agents and casting people don't want to be fooled. An overly madeup, airbrushed photograph that tries to improve on Mother Nature too much is verbotin and sounds a death knell for getting a role.

Remember, actors are cast for a part because they look the part. Whether the performer is, for example, an ingenue, leading man, character actor, or a grandmother type, a good headshot projects who that someone is, not who the person is pretending to be. Young actresses, in particular, can fall into this trap. The "I'm trying to look like Madonna" syndrome is a silly goal when a teenager or young woman doesn't bear much of a resemblance to her. When actors put on too much makeup, wear the wrong clothes, and then have their photographs airbrushed excessively, they're simply adding insult to injury in terms of the casting crowd. Doing this wastes their time because they can tell the minute you walk in that the picture is a phony.

Matthew Mastowski's photograph will open show-business doors quickly because it satisfies all of the requirements for a great headshot: straight-on identification with the viewer, terrific personality projection, and the laid-back charm that is the antithesis of a haughty attitude. This outdoor commercial headshot of Matthew says "real." His understated wardrobe enhances his boyish face. I used a simple white-cardboard reflector to illuminate his features, thereby capitalizing on his healthy appearance.

As a professional headshot photographer, you have a responsibility to your clients. Yes, light your subjects flatteringly, make them up to their best advantage, style their hair carefully—do all that you can to make them look their very best. But don't do any of this to an extreme because you'll be undermining the talents' chances for successful careers in the entertainment field.

After you discuss prices and other details and book a session with clients, the next step is to talk about the wardrobe that they'll bring to the shoot, as well as the various looks that they want you to capture. Ordinarily, I break up the shooting session into four sections, devoting each one to a different look. There are four types of headshots: commercial, legit, industrial, and glamour. Each of these is distinctive and has a specific purpose. Together, they cover all the looks that an aspiring actor needs. You can adapt these four basic shots to both genders, as well as every age group; you simply have to make minor modifications for children.

Matthew
Mastowski

THE COMMERCIAL HEADSHOT

The primary goal of this type of headshot, which has a relaxed, "outdoorsy" feel to it, is personality projection. To help clients relax and reveal their true natures as they sell a product, you must provide a comfortable atmosphere during the shoot. Having a sense of humor is very helpful; it can make your clients feel at ease and can establish a light tone for the creative process. This is where your skills as a director come into play. For example, I sometimes tell clients to look straight into the camera and say something like, "This orange juice is delicious!" By doing this, they start performing—and stop thinking about themselves and how tense they are. The trick is to get them to project the idea that they are happy about the product. They should smile and look friendly. In terms of lighting, I like these lively photographs to be well illuminated and bright in keeping with the mood on the set.

Actors wear casual clothes for commercial headshots. Pastel colors are best for both men and women, as are polo and other open-collared shirts. Blue denim, khaki, and tan also translate well in black and white. Clothes from The Gap and Banana Republic are always appropriate for commercial headshots; the same is true of Nautica's sporty sailing-motif designs. Children and young-looking teenagers can wear outdoor playclothes.

Here you see two commercial headshots that reveal the clients' personalities. When photographing Tom Kulesa, I knew that I had to record his great smile. Directing Tom was a pleasure; with just a few simple instructions, he was able to respond to the camera. His natural charm is evident in this casual outdoors shot, for which he wore an open-collared denim shirt.

Like Tom, Janice Vahl has a sparkling personality. For her commercial headshot, she wore a tailored, light-blue shirt whose collar I turned up just slightly and small gold-loop earrings. Her makeup is minimal, and her short hair doesn't dominate her face or smile. But Janice's eyes are her best feature. They look sincere and suggest that she wants to tell you about a product she is completely satisfied with. The bright, cheery illumination that gradually changes from darker at the top behind Janice's head to lighter just below her neck and shoulders works well here.

Tom Kulesa

Janice Vahl

THE LEGIT HEADSHOT

Although actors ordinarily use this headshot to get parts in the theater, they can also use it for film, soap-opera, and other television-series roles, dramatic or otherwise. The legit shot is quieter and more thoughtful than the commercial shot. Actors look very sincere in their legit headshots and make strong eye contact with the camera. Once again, it is important for you to act like a director. If you supply clients with lines to say to the camera, they'll have to concentrate on their delivery rather than themselves.

Wardrobe for the legit headshot can be a shade darker than the pastels that are appropriate for the commercial shot. Open collars are fine, but actresses may decide to wear flattering scoop necklines. The overwhelming impression legit shots leave is a no-nonsense one. Actors dress many different ways, and respecting their individual styles can help effect the "it looks like them when they walk in" effort. Of course, there is a limit to how bizarre your subjects' clothing can be. Alice Spivak selected a dark V-neck and drop earrings, which dress up her headshot just a bit. Her smile is bit big, but it still falls into the legit-picture range because it is so sincere.

When I discussed June Kesler's shoot with her, we agreed that a somewhat glamorous look would suit her best. She has often played "the other woman," as well as other roles with a "not to be trusted" twist. June did her own gorgeous wavy hair as well as most of her makeup; I simply added the finishing contouring touches. To play up her face and hair, she wore a simple zippered V-neck top. Her controlled smile indicates that this is a legit shot.

Lighting setups for legit shots can include a focused key light that is less bright than that used in commercial headshots, as well as a slightly softer backlight on the subject's hair. Legit lighting is also theatrical because it calls for less fill or reflected light on the performer's face, which in turn reduces the amount of contrast between the subject and the requisite dark background.

Shooting legit shots of children requires special attention. Since these pictures are slightly more serious than commercial shots, getting young subjects to pose for them is easier. Children's clothing doesn't have to be quite so sporty or outdoorsy; you simply have to make sure that the colors won't appear too dark and murky in the final image.

In their legit shots, boys and girls should look fresh and bursting with a child's special energy. Don't let the quiet nature of legit headshots compel you to make images that are too serious.

Alice
Spivak

June Kesler

THE INDUSTRIAL HEADSHOT

Performers need this type of headshot to get work in industrial films, which are promo films companies use either for in-house purposes or for such out-of-house events as trade shows. Because industrial headshots reflect the business world and its way of dressing and behaving, conservative is the watchword here. Consequently, nothing should go far beyond the norms set by the establishment for clothes, accessories, and, in particular, hairstyles and makeup. These headshots are quieter and more intense than the others but are nonetheless friendly.

Men and women of all ages must assume a professional look for an industrial headshot. When you plan this kind of headshot, tell male clients that they should have a suit and tie with them, and tell female clients to bring a blazer or suit jacket and light-colored blouse. Keep in mind, however, that for both the fashion world and the world of design and art direction, clothing for industrial headshots can be a bit dramatic: Ralph Lauren or Calvin Klein instead of Hickey Freeman. And since these rather staid photographs are similar to executive portraits used in annual reports, they should have a sincerity about them. The lighting can be somewhat subdued and minimal in comparison to that used for commercial shots. In addition, some backgrounds can be dark, thereby suggesting a quiet boardroom.

Constance Barron is an ideal representative of the upscale professional woman whose intelligence has enabled her to succeed in the business world. Her clothes are tailored, not glamorous. Connie's relatively simple hairdo and understated makeup also reflect the conservative corporate environment. In terms of jewelry, she wore only tiny earrings. For this industrial shot, I used a very basic lighting pattern, with no excessive backlights or hair lights. The result: a straight-on, personable, but not overly energetic headshot.

Lyle Rose's photograph has all the qualities of a great executive shot. He wore a suit and tie that makes him look very Wall Street here. In addition, Lyle projects a built-in honesty and warmth that comes right off the printed paper. I wanted a simple but effective lighting design for this industrial shot, so I illuminated him straight on without a reflector. A soft rimlight on my subject's hair and shoulders separates him from the mottled background.

Constance Barron

Lyle Rose

THE GLAMOUR HEADSHOT

When posing for a glamour shot, performers can exude some sex appeal because this picture is used for getting work in Hollywood, in clubs, and on soap operas and other television shows, among other venues. While sex appeal is a commodity that actors should never push, they should be aware of it. The simplest way to encourage performers to add some oomph to their glamour headshot is to have them do the old Marlon Brando or Marilyn Monroe "I love you, camera" routine. I tell—and sometimes have to coax—my subjects to concentrate on only the lens and nothing else, just like in a love scene. Of course, I don't want my clients to go too far and end up with a boudoir-photography look, which often goes beyond the boundaries of good taste in terms of sensuality.

Clothes for glamour shots can be a little more expensive looking than they can for other kinds of headshots. You might want to suggest a tuxedo shirt for men and a silk or satin blouse for women. When I photograph cabaret, opera, and musical-comedy singers, I recommend that they wear what they perform in. (Teenagers are generally considered too young for glamour shots.)

Stella Pierce exudes glamour without even trying, from her long hair swept over to one side, to her unusual but effective choice of wardrobe. She wore a gray-velvet vest with cream-satin lapels. Although not every female client can carry off such a dramatic outfit—complete with a pearl necklace—Stella certainly was able to. This shows that she is aware of her strengths and knows how to accentuate them to her advantage. As further proof of this, she did her own makeup. The result: a smashing glamour headshot.

Like Stella, cabaret performer Lydia Gray doesn't have to do anything extraordinary to project a glamorous image; it seems innate. Wearing a strapless black-velvet gown, a double strand of pearls, and pearl earrings, she is the epitome of chic. Lydia's luxurious, dark hair, which she styled, and bright smile add to the appeal of this glamour shot.

Lighting for glamour headshots is quite dramatic and results in an "in the spotlight" feeling. For some clients, I even use soft focus to achieve the "stars in the eyes" effect. And to simulate a music-video look, I illuminate the hair with a strong, hot backlight.

When you discuss the various headshot possibilities that you can create with potential clients, they'll get excited about the looks that are available to them. By being enthusiastic about your work, you can impress actors with your familiarity with and knowledge of what you're trying to do for them in their headshots. As a result, they are much more likely to book with you! And keep in mind that subjects know instinctively whether or not a photographer has the background needed to take great pictures of them.

LYDIA GRAY

Stella Pierce

CHAPTER ONE

THE BUSINESS OF PHOTOGRAPHING PROFESSIONAL HEADSHOTS

A working professional actor needs the very best professional headshots that will elicit a positive response from casting agents and directors. If you want to be one of the top headshot photographers, you need to be an expert with your camera and lighting equipment and to make the professional needs of the performers who come to you for superlative headshots your primary concern. You must be involved with who they are, what they want, and where they're planning on going in the entertainment world.

In New York City alone, there are dozens of headshot photographers. Just pick up a copy of *Backstage*, the actor's weekly newspaper for casting calls and other important information, and you'll see many headshot photographers' advertisements. Like the photographers themselves, some ads are terrific, some are good, some are average, and some are on the level of passport photographers. If you want to succeed in this business and stand out from the competition, you must produce top-notch photographs that portray clients in a vital, attractive way. This informal shot of Kevin vanHentenryck reflects his easygoing nature and appealing good looks.

In order to capture your clients' personality on film, you have to see the very best in them when they come to your studio for headshots. It is good business practice to compliment your clients as you begin to work together. For example, you may tell a younger leading man that he reminds you of Kevin Costner or Denzel Washington. By having clients keep a stellar model in mind as they pose, you're immediately setting a very high standard for the shoot. Since you're putting your clients on a pedestal from the start, the session will go better and the results

will be even more spectacular than expected. Sincere flattery at the onset of your professional relationship with your client can be quite beneficial, whether you're dealing with new talent or people who are already in the business.

I have to continue to earn praise every time I work with a client. Establishing a good reputation is critical if you hope to make money shooting headshots. This is hard work, and you really have to care about the people who come to you. After all, these aspiring actors are putting their careers in your hands, and you're striving to continue yours.

Kevin vanHentenryck

WHAT ACTORS LOOK FOR

How do actors select the right headshot photographer for their needs? What criteria do they use to choose the headshot photographer who will help turn them into stars, or at the very least working professionals? All potential clients require a headshot that represents them in a professional way. They want to look like themselves, but themselves at their best.

If actors aren't familiar with a photographer's work, they need to set up an appointment for an interview to see the photographer's portfolio, which contains examples of his or her best work. If during the interview the actors have a basic, positive response to the style of the headshot samples, they'll start asking such pertinent questions as "How many rolls of film do you shoot?" and "How much does your package cost, and how many enlargements are included?"

When you discuss these options, you must remember that you're dealing with actors who hope to become stars and whose express purpose in life is to work in the acting profession. As a headshot photographer, you should respect and cater to this strong influence on their lives; you should also remember that show-business clients typically differ in look and temperament from average citizens. If a rapport between the actor and the photographer develops, the performer may book a firm appointment for a headshot photo session. Depending on the individual photographer's business style, a deposit to secure that particular time slot in the appointment calendar may be requested at this point.

The next decision involves the different types of shots that will be taken. This determines the kind of clothing the actor will bring to the shoot, such as sporty weekend outfits, a business suit, or, perhaps, even a tuxedo. When I met with Agostino Profumo, we decided on four headshots of him in casual clothes to

Agostino Profumo

show off his dark, handsome features. The resulting composite is a winner.

Many actors often stay with a headshot for a year or two and then have new shots taken to update their image. Later sessions proceed more smoothly than initial shoots because both the photographer and client are more at ease, the small talk flows more readily, and a comfortable rapport develops more quickly. Establishing an excellent working relationship with each person is important in terms of repeat business. These new shots also give actors the opportunity to re-spark the interest of agents and casting directors.

POTENTIAL CLIENTS

As a headshot photographer, you'll be working with a diverse group of clientele. For example, you may find yourself photographing business executives who need a publicity shot for newspapers, magazines, and annual reports. Before you agree to shoot an executive portrait, keep in mind that this often entails leaving your studio and going to the executive's office. Another potential drawback is that most executives have a short attention span; they have more serious business to attend to and want to get the photo session over quickly. As a result, photographers ordinarily use less film for these type of shots than they do for others. The trick with executive shots is to get your subjects to relax and look friendly. Since an executive portrait takes less time than an actor's headshots do, I charge less for the session.

Other potential clients include a couple who is planning to get married and wants an engagement shot. I try to infuse this often boring type of shot with some show-business glamour and vitality to make it come alive. I dislike engagement pictures that seem to suggest that the couple is thinking twice about tying the knot. A wedding-announcement shot is relatively simple to do because my subjects bring only one change of clothes and need only one shot, so I charge them my lower headshot fee.

You'll find, however, that actors and other performers will provide your main source of income, and they need a much broader variety of images than the executive and the happy couple do. Furthermore, actors have at their disposal a varied range of feelings that they can project. In fact, since performers have so many emotions and expressions that they can tap into, you'll be able to choose only a few to shoot. It is up to you to get your subjects to focus on one emotion at a time. Fortunately, actors are used to taking direction, so guiding them throughout the headshot session shouldn't cause any problems.

John Miller, a talented musician, wanted a laid-back image for his legit headshot. To achieve this, he wore a plaid sweater over a light-toned, button-down shirt; smiled warmly; and gazed right into the camera. I then directed him to tilt his head down to avoid reflections in his eyeglasses.

Providing potential clients with this information during the interview will reassure them. I mention that I'll even give them copy, or lines, to say to the camera. This approach gives the final photographs more sparkle and personality and convinces the actors that they'll be in good hands during what many of them consider to be a trying situation. Show-business clientele are very special—and sometimes very insecure—people. They come to you with their hearts in their hands, asking for good headshots. Their very careers depend on their glossies, so you must give them your very best shot!

JOHN
MILLER

THE INTERVIEW

Whenever you want to get to know someone new, especially if you feel that a person can help your career, you have to arrange a meeting first. During the initial meeting with a portrait photographer, actors get to see the quality of the headshots. They also learn whether or not they'll be able to work with the photographer. As such, when potential clients arrive at your studio for the first time, it is important that they immediately get the sense that you're concerned about their individual characteristics and personalities. Make sure that the images you show them are samples of your best work and capture the subjects' uniqueness. Whether you display these headshots on a gallery-like arrangement on a wall or in a portfolio, you should select pictures with a diversity of expressions, lighting setups, and moods, all of which show the subjects at their best.

Here you see the promotional composite that I had printed for my studio. I balanced the freewheeling, smiling shots with the glamour shot in the lower right-hand corner, thereby achieving the needed variety of images. Placing a shot of Jeff Daniels, a well-known actor, in the upper right-hand corner draws the viewers' eye. It takes a great deal of thought and imagination to put together an effective showcase of your most dynamic shots to promote your skills.

Most actors interview six or seven photographers before they decide which one they'll hire. If potential clients look at a photographer's images and say to themselves, "All of these people look the same," they probably won't hire that photographer. But if potential clients like the work—and like the photographer—even after they've seen the pictures of several others, it is time to set up an appointment. The next step is to ask for a deposit in order to clinch the verbal contract and to "hold that particular time for the client." Remember, accepting a deposit is a binding procedure.

You must then determine how much you're going to charge clients. I suggest starting out with a reasonable fee, around perhaps 75 to 100 dollars. Then after a year or two of satisfying customers and perfecting your style and technique, raise your fee to about 150 dollars. As your reputation and expertise build, you can increase your prices gradually.

Some photographers charge clients about 600 dollars. This figure often includes 100 dollars for the hairstylist and another 100 dollars for the makeup person. I charge 300 dollars; this price includes the makeup application, which I most often do myself. The package also covers the three 36-exposure rolls of 35mm film that I shoot and three 8 x 10 enlargements.

I charge clients who are younger than 16 a fee of 250 dollars in order to give parents, who usually pay for the session, a needed break. The slight difference with this package is that I shoot only two 36-exposure rolls of film and provide two 8 x 10 glossies.

A final note on prices. Actors' newspapers, such as *Backstage* and *New York Casting*, carry advertisements that offer different deals. One photographer charges just 49 dollars for headshots, while another photographer says that the shoot costs nothing if you don't like the pictures. Still another photographer might claim that you pay for the enlargements only, but the price of each of these is probably inflated. I've even come across an ad in which a photographer would allow you to take your own picture at his "studio." I am sure that the results would look as professional as shots taken in a booth at a shopping mall or in front of a passport-photo setup.

Actors don't get good parts if they promote themselves with a cheap-looking headshot. Headshot photographers should want their clients to look like potential top-notch stars, not rank amateurs. This is where a responsible headshot photographer excels or falls short because, as always, quality shows on any level. Give your clients the best quality and your very best work, which is what they deserve.

New York's Leading Head Shot Photographer ...among the most respected names in lighting today... Author of... 50 Portrait Lighting Techniques for Pictures That Sell -Billboard Publications, 1983 john hart (212) 873-6585

MAKEUP AND HAIRSTYLING RECOMMENDATIONS

Hair and makeup are essential ingredients that give performers a "ready-for-camera" appearance. If you and your clients don't pay attention to or care about how the skin and hair look, the effect in the final image can seem raw, unfinished, and unprofessional. Believe it or not, everyone needs makeup, no matter how minimal; I even have to lighten the under-the-eye area on seven-year-old children because just about everyone goes a tad dark there.

Of course, you must strike the delicate balance between too much and too little. Makeup and hairstyles in professional headshots should never be extreme. What looks good on camera is the paramount consideration here. The makeup for leading men or male executives shouldn't overpower the individuals; it should enhance their features. Leading ladies, though, are expected to wear a great deal of makeup, a standard Hollywood established years ago. In fact, an actress's complexion should photograph one or two shades lighter than that of the actor playing opposite her in a scene.

I ordinarily tell clients of both sexes that I'll do their makeup on the day of the shoot; I keep a full supply of makeup at my studio. When clients and I agree that I'm going to do the makeup, I ask them to bring their own makeup if they have any allergies. However, if my client hires someone else to apply the makeup either before the session or at my studio, I insist on being the final arbiter of what will look good under the lights and in the lens. As you can see in this shot, client Joanna Sly is preparing for her session, and Krista Lorn, the woman she hired to do her makeup and hair, is adding the finishing touches. Once I approved Krista's work, I began shooting. I keep up with the latest trends in makeup, which come and go with each and every fashion cycle. One season matte lipstick and lots of mascara are in vogue, and the next season, glossy lipstick and little mascara are the style. I also apply makeup in the most flattering way possible to make my clients look their very best.

Hairstyles should also fall in the middle range and not be too simple or elaborate. For women, the hair should look styled but not too busy. It also should be brushed back and away from the face rather than piled on top of the head. For men, medium-length-hair is the best choice for professional headshots. For children, medium-length hair is ideal, and the style shouldn't feature long bangs or be very curly.

There are exceptions, of course, such as rock musicians and singers who usually wear their hair long so they can throw it around during a performance. Some clients who want to get into modeling may ask for the wet look; here, I simply wet the hair and tousle it a bit or brush it back with my fingers. Finally, some younger clients may want to apply a lot of styling gel to their hair. This is fine for a few headshots, but you should shoot some variations as well.

Most casting people prefer to see a client's hair shaped to the contours of the individual's face. The hair should be professionally styled, of course, yet it shouldn't be so curly and wavy that it becomes a distraction. If clients want a hairstylist to come to the studio and work with them, I can recommend someone. If they want to go to their own stylist before the shoot, that is fine, as is styling their hair themselves in an acceptable way.

Finally, it is good idea to have a checklist of what you should have on hand and what must be done on the day of the shoot. For example, you'll need facial and eye makeup in a wide variety of colors, sponges, hair dryers, curling irons and brushes, combs and hairbrushes, mousses, gels, hairsprays, cotton swabs, and tissues. You must also make sure that the changing room is neat and clean and that all of the makeup and hairstyling tools you'll need are organized and readily accessible.

DEALING WITH CLIENTS

Although many photographers attend various fine schools across the country, photography classes alone don't adequately prepare novice portrait photographers. Ideally, a headshot photographer's classes should include basic training in psychology, art direction, fashion, makeup, styling, and some medicine. Professional portrait photographers must be able to handle the seemingly endless range of personalities, attitudes, emotional responses, and major and minor neuroses of the spectrum of clients who come to them for photographs. In addition, subjects can be anywhere from nine months old to 90 years old, and this also demands adaptability on the part of the photographer.

The more you shoot, the more you'll appreciate ideal clients. They have their wardrobe planned ahead of time, know exactly how they want their hair and makeup to look, arrive on time, and are in a terrific mood while working in the studio. Brian Thurston, for example, proved to be a wonderful client. He came prepared to work with me to produce winning headshots, like the legit shot you see here. He made great eye contact with the lens throughout the session, and his wardrobe choices showed off his good looks to their best advantage.

Most clients, however, arrive for the photo session feeling quite insecure. As a result, they may be difficult to work with and have an attitude. Your first job, naturally, is to bolster your subjects' self-confidence. All performers don't like something about themselves, no matter how attractive they are. They might not be happy with the shape of their nose or jaw line or the clothes that they brought to the session, or they might not like their complexion, hairstyle, or teeth. Perhaps they simply didn't get a good night's sleep. You must then reassure your clients that they do indeed look terrific.

Still other actors may arrive at your studio feeling quite tense and stressed out for a number of reasons. For example, a cab might have taken them out of the way, their hairdresser did a poor job, a child might not like having his picture taken, a teenager might be having trouble with his self-image, or a 20-year-old might be upset that she is no longer 19. Obviously, you must be prepared to provide whatever emotional balms your clients need.

The most important weapon you have to battle any and all of these diverse insecurities is the ability to get your subjects to relax. This is no easy task sometimes. You can start by greeting them at the studio with a warm, friendly smile. "If I'm relaxed, they'll be relaxed" should be your dictum. Next, you can ask them how they feel, comment on how great they look, and ask if they would like a cup of coffee.

First and foremost, though, you must assure them that there is absolutely no rush. You're going to take your time and ease them into the situation. You must also be excited about the session since clients will pick up on your enthusiasm. After all, a successful portrait session must have a good energy level. And once you get the performers to concentrate on the business at hand, such as their wardrobe and makeup, they'll leave their insecurities behind in the change room.

When all the preliminary work is done, you can begin concentrating on directing your clients. This is an important skill for headshot photographers to have. Not only are actors used to taking direction, they almost demand it. They want to feel a sense of security about what they're doing. To facilitate this, you can help them decide what each character they're playing is doing and saying at a particular time. Then tell them to imagine that they are this person and to talk right into the camera, making comments that are appropriate to the role and situation. This helps actors get into character and gives each wardrobe change its own emotional reality. Be sure to explore various possibilities with your subjects and to try different approaches. Fortunately, most clients are grateful to work with a photographer whose primary purpose is to provide them with fabulous headshots; consequently, they'll be amenable to that pro's direction and expertise.

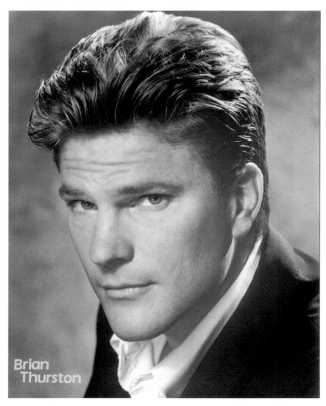

Brian Thurston

ORGANIZING YOUR STUDIO SPACE

Ideally, a photographer's studio is large, bright, airy, and carefully appointed with the amenities that potential clients expect to see in a neat, well-run professional environment. But this dream studio may be down the line for photographers relatively new to the headshot business. If you're just getting your career started and must work at home, you need to establish a space strictly for your photography. Clear out the sofa, end tables, and floor lamps so that you'll have at least one entire room set aside as studio space. If taking over the living room is impossible, consider converting the garage or a spare bedroom.

Wherever you decide to set up your makeshift studio, be sure to thoroughly clean the area and paint it photographer white. This will create a professional look and will make you feel more competent, too. Don't start out photographing people in a corner of your living or dining room after hanging up a roll of white background paper; this looks tacky and will never enable you to reach the upper echelon of portrait photography.

A professional-looking studio has a separate reception area where you can greet your guests, even if this is simply the front hall. Since you might be working with children accompanied by a parent or guardian, you should make the reception area as roomy as possible. The reception area is also the place where you'll show potential clients samples of your work. As mentioned earlier, you can hang these first-rate headshots on a wall or collect them in a portfolio.

Keep in mind, however, that no matter how many photographs you have on the wall, some clients will invariably ask to see your portfolio. Because of this, I have four separate portfolios, one for actors, one for actresses, one for executives, and one for composites. Whichever way you decide to show your work, select your very best images, shots that contain a variety of expressions, moods, and lighting designs so that the pictures don't all look the same. Furthermore, if you hope to concentrate on a specific subject, such as children, you should feature photographs of them.

In terms of the physical layout, a beginning studio should be equipped with several chairs, a stool, two basic lighting setups, different shades of background paper, and, if possible, three or four foamcore panels of varying textures and reflective surfaces. You might want to consider a brushed-aluminum look, a flat-gray color, or a faux-canvas surface that you can paint. Simply stipple or spray various neutral colors on the surface, and be sure to blend them softly. You must, of course, make sure that the backgrounds you choose aren't so interesting that they become distractions and shift attention away from the face or figure in the foreground. For example, don't place bold stripes, squares, or circular designs in the background. They don't retreat or blend in behind the subject.

The front bathroom in my studio is large and has high ceilings, so it makes a great changing room where the talent can hang up their clothes, relax, and get ready for the shoot. The lights over the sink are perfect

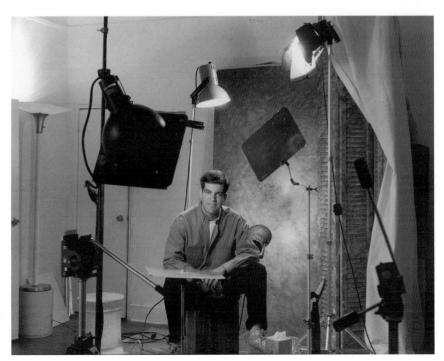

for makeup application and hairstyling, and there are numerous outlets to accommodate hair dryers, curling irons, and hot rollers. The availability of a changing room gives your subjects a chance to get some much-needed privacy during the session, which in turn provides them with a sense of security. If your studio space doesn't allow for a separate changing room, you can set up a couple of folding tan or white canvas panels behind which your subjects can get dressed. You can also use these panels as backdrops.

PHOTOGRAPHIC EQUIPMENT

If photographers want to work exclusively with natural outdoor light, they'll need only a white reflector or fill-flash. But if they want to photograph clients in a studio situation, then they'll need some primary lighting equipment. Two basic lighting setups dominate the professional-headshot business. One approach calls for hot lights. This is a generic term for incandescent light sources, such as common household 25-, 60-, and 100-watt light bulbs. Portrait photography requires much hotter lights with a much higher wattage in order to achieve brighter, sharper images. In the studio, I use hot lights that give me a full spread of light, like the kind of illumination that pours into a room from an open window. These lights are called *floods* or *fresnels*. Conversely, *spotlights* are more concentrated and focused lights that enable photographers to isolate a specific area or face.

Today, floods and spotlights are often powered by intense but long-lasting halogen-quartz lamps that put out from 300 to several thousand watts of light. These floods and spots can be interchanged. In addition, they are mobile enough so that you can move them around as main lights or *backlights* as much as your portrait needs demand. For a main, or key, light, I use a flood called a *scoop light*. Its large, 500-watt quartz light is placed next to the back of a bowl-like metal unit, thereby throwing a great deal of soft light on the subject's face. For a backlight or *hair light*, I use either a tall spotlight or two smaller 150-watt incandescent floods to highlight the back of my client's hair. For *reflected light*, which is the *fill* or *bounce light* that augments the main facial light on a client, I use an aluminum rectangle.

Halogen-tungsten lights, on the other hand, aren't needed for backlighting. Although they are smaller coil

lamps, the intense heat that they provide is too hot for backlighting. A 150-watt spotlight or flood offers adequate illumination here. After all, you don't want the light on the background to be stronger than the light on the subject's face.

The other primary lighting arrangement calls for strobe lights. These synched flash units fire at mere thousands of a watt-seconds. As such, strobes have the ability to stop a basketball player or a ballet dancer in midair. These lights were developed initially for stop-motion photography and later applied to fashion photography. They eliminated fashion shots with blurred images of models, hair, and fabrics.

And since these flash units are cool and seem to never wear out, they have an advantage over hot lights; however, I think that you can more effectively finesse light and shade with hot lights than with strobes. Because strobe lights are bounced into umbrellas, the resulting illumination is simply too flat for headshots. It lacks the modeled lighting effects of the hot-light sources used for theater, television, and film.

Both hot lights and strobes can have *barndoors*, which are four black rectangles attached to the front of the unit. These flexible doors help to focus the light on the desired area. This, in turn, keeps the strong flashes of the two light sources from spilling over onto sections of the shooting area that you don't want to emphasize.

These two lighting styles have different and distinctive looks. I prefer using studio hot lights for a simple reason. Actors work under these types of lights—spotlights, scoop lights, and floods—in various show-business venues throughout their career. They seem to come alive while they are under the spotlight. As such, I think it is important to use this kind of illumination for their headshots. Furthermore, I believe that all you need to produce good headshots is one key light, one hair light, and one reflector. Sometimes I add a backlight, but often there is enough spill light from the other lights to illuminate the background. Also, if you tilt a 4 x 8-foot sheet of aluminum-covered foamcore toward the backdrop, this reflects enough light so that a background light isn't needed. You can better bring out the nuances of bone structure than you can by using the more intense bounce light of a strobe-lighting setup. These lights also requires more retouching than hot lights do.

If you are seriously interested in becoming a portrait photographer, you can buy these various lights at any legitimate photo-supply store. Renting these pieces of equipment isn't cost effective over the long run. The following is a list of the lighting equipment that I have in my studio.

1 650-watt scoop light with barndoors to modulate amount of light on subject

1 650-watt spotlight with four barndoors to flood the subject's hair with backlighting

2 150-watt Smith-Victor floods to softly backlight the subject's hair

1 150-watt flood to provide fill light for the subject's face (an alternate to an aluminum reflector)

1 600-watt halogen-quartz Lowell Tota Light to provide fill light for the studio, for three-quarter-length and full-length shots

1 black flag on a stand in front of and to the right or left of the camera to block strong backlight from entering the camera lens

1 aluminum reflector on a stand to bounce light into the subject's face and to soften shadows created by the main light

  Filters of various thicknesses to control the intensity of the lights

Of course, an individual photographer's taste greatly influences the decision to use hot lights or strobe lights. While I ordinarily opt for hot lights, I sometimes use my Norman strobe-lighting setup, particularly when I shoot color. When working with my Norman 1200 watt-second strobe, I split up the unit's power three ways. I designate 800 watt-seconds for the key umbrella bounce light, 200 watt-seconds for the hair light, and 200 watt-seconds for the background light. You can, of course, vary the power breakdowns. You can even buy several powerpacks of 1000 watt-seconds each, which comes in handy when you photograph more than one person in action. Strobe is certainly great for stop-action photography because it enables you to shoot at shutter speeds of 1/1000 sec. Bouncing a main light into an umbrella results in less light from the flash because one-third of the illumination is absorbed, so you must take a meter reading off the light source.

Whichever type of lighting you decide on, keep in mind that when you photograph performers, especially those who are used to working one-on-one with an audience, it is important to give them as much freedom of movement as possible within the lighting-setup area. Strobe lights make this easier to achieve than hot lights do, but the choice is ultimately yours. As a headshot photographer, your main concern is to capture those magic moments when your clients reveal their personality during a given shoot.

LIGHTING ON LOCATION

In addition to using artificial light in the studio, you can leave your studio and go on location to shoot outdoors in natural or available light. I find shooting outside is actually easier than shooting in the studio because it requires far less equipment. I bring only a white reflector board with me and rely on the sun to provide the illumination, overcast or not. For example, if I want to make head-and-shoulders shots in shade, I simply position my subjects so that they face the sun and eliminate any distracting background elements.

Although outdoor headshots aren't popular with some casting people on the East Coast, I think that if an outdoor setting brings out a performer's personality in the very best way, you should shoot there. And working outside before shooting in the studio often relaxes clients. There is something about the outdoors that immediately puts people at ease and subsequently helps them work well during a trying situation.

Since so many commercials are shot on location, I feel that working outdoors is particularly effective for commercial headshots. I can usually balance the natural appeal of commercial headshots done outside with the more designed look of shots made in the studio. Then when I review both sets of pictures with clients, we can still narrow down our favorite three photographs from the more than 100 shots taken inside and out. In any case, I rarely do an entire shoot outdoors; ordinarily, I shoot one roll of film outside and the other two in the studio.

No matter what lighting design you use, it is an unalterable fact that actors can hope to get work in the entertainment industry only when they circulate a headshot that portrays them as who they intrinsically are, not who they might be pretending to be. Projecting this basic honesty in a professional headshot is what makes a headshot great.

ADVERTISING AND MARKETING YOUR WORK

In order to compete successfully in this exciting headshot-photography market, you need to take advantage of the various advertising techniques available. The basic way to promote your skills is to advertise in the actors' newspapers published weekly. In New York City, you can advertise in the tried-and-true *Backstage* and the newer *New York Casting Guide*; in Los Angeles, you can place an ad in *Drama/Logue*. Running an ad in any or all of these publications, as well as the nationally known *Variety* and *The Hollywood Reporter* will surely result in some telephone calls about your portrait/headshot photography. And, naturally, you'll be ready to follow up your advertising and marketing claims with an excellent portfolio.

The advertisements that I've placed in *Backstage* were included on the "Casting Page," which is where most actors look for audition material. My ads contain my logo, which is my actual signature, as the graphic grabber. The subheads read either "Takes the best headshots, naturally," or "New York's top headshot photographer." I also mention one of my previous books for Amphoto, *50 Portrait Lighting Techniques for Pictures That Sell*, and include my telephone number. I always use a photograph in my ad, too. Sometimes I choose an actress, other times I decide to go with an actor, and still other times I use a combination.

And like many other photographers who do what I do, I advertise in *The Backstage Handbook for the Performing Artist*, which is put out by the publishers of *Backstage*. Another annual publication that is a good resource is *New York Casting and Survival Guide*, from Peter Glenn Publications. I tried advertising in national magazines, but I never got quite the response that I did with ads appearing in local media.

In addition, appearing on a radio- or television-interview show can help spread the word about your studio, too. Truly exploiting major media markets, however, requires a good public-relations person. Although their services aren't cheap, you might want to seriously consider hiring one. A public-relations person charges minimally 100 dollars a week.

Marketing your work is a job in itself. To help you get started, I suggest that you read *Marketing Warfare* by Trout and Reis. I occasionally have lunch with an agent who happens to be a friend and recommends me to clients. I also send postcards throughout the year and do a big mailing during the holiday season. My largest postcard mentions the television shows that I've been a guest on. To save yourself a great deal of time and effort when you do a mailing of cards and letters, buy a set of gummed labels printed with the names and addresses of all the production companies, casting agencies, talent agents, unions, and television shows. You can find these mailing labels at specialty bookstores, such as Applause in New York City. A booklet called *Ross Reports, NYC*, also lists all of the above companies.

Publicity releases are another means of marketing your skills. It is important to keep your name circulating in the entertainment world as much as possible. I've tried to coordinate my cards, envelopes, and stationery for a polished, professional look. I also repeat both my name and logo as much as possible in my advertisements and promotional material so that it is an easily identifiable symbol.

PHOTOGRAPHING CHILDREN

In the last few years, children have become more and more visible in the entertainment industry. They've been featured in blockbuster Steven Spielberg, Sylvester Stallone, and Arnold Schwarzenegger movies; in soap operas; and, as always, in numerous commercials. Today, children even have their very own television station, Nickelodeon, in addition to all of the shows geared toward them on other stations. Clearly, this burgeoning market dealing with young talent can be an extra source of income for headshot photographers. In order to attract this set as clients, put together a portfolio of your best shots of children and make the rounds of managers and agents who handle young talent exclusively, such as All American Talent in New York City and Ford Kids. Be aware that it takes awhile for agents to have confidence in your work; however, the additional income can be satisfying. Also, you can advertise that you specialize in younger-talent headshot photography.

To successfully work with children, you need to keep in mind what might seem to an obvious statement: Their responses to direction and their attitudes can vary from those of adults. Because of their lack of experience with the shooting process, they require a bit more patience than adults do; they're also easily distracted. Stay calm, and don't be too dictatorial. This can make them start to pout and get upset.

You need to respect your young subjects' moods as you try to elicit the same basic range of emotions as you do with older clients. You want to capture them looking both happy and somewhat serious. But the most important picture you'll take is a fun-filled, smiling commercial headshot because this is the photograph that will generate most of their work.

Telling children to pretend that they're doing a commercial for McDonald's or that they're talking to Big Bird to get them to look into the camera. You have to help them relax and have a good time during the session. You might also want to keep some props around, such as a giant crayon, to act as tension breakers. It is also important for you to establish a good rapport with the parent or guardian who accompanies a child to a shoot. This is critical because children immediately pick up on the kind of communication going on between

adults. Fuss over the children and the parents when they arrive. Make them feel at home. Children respond favorably when adults are in a good mood. This added sense of security will, in turn, make the shoot enjoyable for everyone involved. Naturally, if you like to photograph children, you'll find that they can be terrific to work with.

Keep in mind that your young subjects have to like you, too, even if you are the director. Be their friend, and let them know that you are on their side. Children have tremendous energy, but you have to get them to focus that excitement in front of the camera.

Photographing Rachel Miner, a talented young soap-opera actress, was a pleasure. She and I have worked together for several years, so she is used to methods and responds accordingly; she is uninhibited and straightforward. For this friendly commercial headshot, Rachel wore a lace top. Her mother brushed her hair back so that its length wouldn't take anything away from her smile. A smidgen of lip gloss was added to provide some contrast to her light skin tone. Makeup, of course, was also low key; I used a medium-tone powder base and a rose blush very sparingly. I chose a neutral-gray background in order to bring out the blondeness of her hair.

Rachel Miner

WARDROBE RECOMMENDATIONS

Like adults, young clients need three or four changes of clothes for the shooting session. The outfits should vary in style and be appropriate for the different shots you'll be taking. Be aware, however, that most parents bring too many clothes because they can't make up their minds and ask you to help them with the final selection. Many parents also want their child to wear all the outfits they own, but you must take charge and refuse their pleas. If you don't, you'll be shooting all day.

In terms of wardrobe recommendations for children, the main consideration is the tops they wear. Although some agents and managers are going along with the current trend for three-quarter-length shots, most still prefer head-and-shoulder shots. Coordinating shirts or blouses and jeans in denim shades or pants work well. Since headshots and composites are black and white, I tell parents that light shades of clothing, such as off-white, tan, and pastels, photograph best. I suggest that they think of styles from The Gap clothing stores. For example, a jean jacket worn over a white, open-collared T-shirt always looks terrific and suggests a relaxed, western feeling. Simply avoid busy logos and lettering on T-shirts and sweatshirts, which can be distracting elements. I recommend an at-play or weekend look for headshots of children. Young talent should come across on film as alive and energetic. Incidentally, casting agents don't want a dressy, going-to-a-formal-party effect. When working with young girls, advise against too-cute hats, as well as distracting stripes, plaids, and floral patterns that can draw attention to themselves.

A brief note about makeup application and hairstyling for children. Boys require less attention than girls do. In fact, I ordinarily use makeup only on boys with a bad complexion. And if a boy's hair isn't rock-star length or cropped in a very short crew cut, you won't have a problem. Makeup application and hairstyling are a bit more involved for girls. You should, however, keep both

to a minimum. Remember, the casual look is most appropriate for children.

Nine-year-old Dina Marie is the youngest stand-up comic in the business. By telling her that I'd attempted some stand-up work along the way the moment she arrived at my studio with her mother, I put her at ease from the start. This also inspired her to have confidence in me, as did seeing shots of children in her age range. For this headshot, I decided not to shoot the big-smile shot usually associated with comedians, but to go with a less pushy and obvious approach. She wore a simple top and matching headband and small earrings. Then by letting Dina Marie perform for her audience, the camera, I was able to capture the quiet, self-confidence that spells professionalism.

DinaMarie

DEALING WITH YOUNG TALENT

While teaching fifth and sixth graders in private and public schools in New York and Indiana, I learned that you must treat any child with the same respect you would give an adult. After all, children are human beings, too, with the same emotional and intellectual needs as adults, only on a less mature level. Your approach must be based on understanding, and you should communicate with them on a one-to-one level, as I did with adorable Ashley Muller. The result: a legit shot showing an impish grin. Children want to be noticed and flattered, too. Use their first name when you greet them and shake their hand (if they are beyond the toddler stage). Let them know that they should feel comfortable and can have some fun during the shooting session.

You should modify this "making a fuss" approach when photographing professional working children who have some experience in the entertainment business. In many situations, the parents have done more than enough flattering. If a subject seems excessively spoiled, your sense of humor will be doubly important as a way to relax the child. Don't take the session so seriously that you appear tense; your mood will inevitably rub off on the child.

Furthermore, in today's cost-conscious show-business arena, producers and directors must adhere to a very tight schedule and don't have time to deal with recalcitrant or difficult children. As a result, they won't last in the job; they can be replaced with other children who are easier to get along with and follow direction without having temper tantrums. When working professionally, children (and adults) are supposed to arrive on the set, follow directions, go home, study their lines for the next day, and arrive prepared. You can expect your clients, young and old alike, to behave and act in a responsible, thoughtful manner. This sense of professionalism should be reflected in a client's headshot. After all, there is a great deal of competition in the world of entertainment, even in the young-talent pool.

Ashley Muller

DIRECTING YOUNG TALENT

When photographing young subjects, you must instruct them to concentrate and to communicate directly with the lens. They should treat the portrait lens as if it were a person they like or perhaps even love. This will prevent them from being distracted. When working with very young talent, I ask the parents to stand right next to the camera because this is where the children's gaze will fall. And having some toy or props around often makes youngsters feel at home.

When children are 10 and older, I diplomatically ask the parents to wait in an adjacent room or at least on the far side of the studio. I find that older children concentrate better when their parents aren't around. In addition, parents often try to elicit their child's favorite expression while I'm trying to shoot, which I find quite distracting. Although I may ask parents to wait off set, I sometimes ask mothers to help with makeup, hair, and wardrobe as the session progresses. I want them to feel like a part of the creative process rather than like an outsider. And don't be intimidated by the stage-mother cliché. Listen to what your clients' mothers have to say, and follow any advice that seems useful. Then go about your business. It is important for you to work with the

mothers, but you shouldn't let them dominate the proceedings. They'll usually respect your authority. Because they want the best for their talented children, they'll bow to your knowledge about the best way to achieve this goal.

Maria Mauro, who is seven years old, has already done some commercials and print modeling. I wanted this headshot to reflect her easygoing personality. Her floral-trimmed blouse provided this casual picture with a pleasing pattern. Directing Maria was almost effortless. I simply asked her to rest her hands and chin on her raised knee. As you can see in this headshot, she felt completely comfortable during the shoot and took instruction well.

Maria Mauro

ONE GIRL, TWO LOOKS

Why are children sometimes photographed looking sad and withdrawn? I think that they are too young to appear to be upset in their images, which are supposed to show them at their best. I try to capture the joy and vitality of youth when I shoot children's headshots.

During every session with children, I also always aim for a diversity of shots. After recording all of the smiles and exuberance required for the commercial shot, I tackle the quieter legit shot; this entails a "going for the eyes" approach. Nevertheless, a legit shot of a child doesn't have to be somber. I dislike intensely pictures of young children who look as though they just lost their favorite puppy.

To get my young subjects to respond appropriately, I have them speak directly to their friend, the camera. For example, I might tell them to say something as simple as, "You're very nice." Otherwise, I might offer a compliment, such as "That's a very nice top you're wearing," and then direct them to answer, "Thank you very much." This picture-taking method enables both my subjects and me to time those magic moments that photographers are always trying to capture on film.

I photographed Christina Scotti on a beautiful sunny day in the park. Susan, her mother, applied a minimal amount of makeup, helped with wardrobe changes, wielded the everpresent hairbrush for touchups, and held the reflector. Here you see two different looks for Christina. For her commercial headshot, she wore a sleeveless denim top and gave me a nice smile (top). Then for her legit shot, I decided to do a three-quarter-length view (bottom). After Christina put on a dark jacket, I directed her to lean against a wall and tip her head down a bit. She looks serious but casual, thanks in part to placing her hands in her pockets. Christina is a real charmer, and once she mastered the "eye-contact trick," she was a breeze to work with. Her headshots project a buoyant, fresh, and full-of-life image, and are so much more vital than typical studio shots.

Christina Scotti

SHOOTING AN OUTDOOR LOOK IN THE STUDIO

Headshot photographers are often asked to do composites, which consist of two or more pictures taken during the photo shoot. For this composite of Marissa C. Bregman, a sports-minded girl who loves to ride horses, her mother and I felt that an outdoor mood would be the best choice. I decided on a combination of one large commercial shot with two smaller shots to show three different styles. These spelled sun, sky, highlighted hair, and freshness. To enhance this effect, we chose a Chanel medium-tone powder for Marissa's base and a Chanel deep-pink blush to add a bit of an outdoor glow to her complexion.

For the large commercial headshot, which serves as the main shot in the composite, Marissa wore a faux-jewel-encrusted denim jacket that makes its own statement (left). But its open collar and the white polo shirt soften its impact. Here, Marissa pulled her hair back to establish a "Hi, how are you?" friendliness.

For the legit shot, Marissa changed into a simple cream-colored top (top right). I then asked her to let her hair fall to its full length and positioned the fan so that it blew her hair back a bit. This reinforced the idea of being outdoors. Marissa's expression here is soft, with just a hint of a Mona Lisa smile to balance the larger smile in the main shot. For another variation, Marissa changed into a pink gingham shirt with an open collar, and her mother tied her hair back with just one striped bow (bottom right). My young subject then flashed a beautiful smile. I made all of Marissa's shots with my Nikon 105mm portrait lens, exposing for 1/60 sec. at f/5.6-8. The background surface was Mylar on foamcore.

Marissa C. Bregman

CHARMERS

Children should look as bright and happy as possible in their commercial headshots. Like their older counterparts, they have personality to sell and project. I don't even mind if they giggle a lot while I photograph them. Of course, working with them outdoors is a better choice than shooting in the studio is. Outside, children feel free, energetic, playful, eager, and relaxed. Most don't have a worry in the world. Furthermore, your young subjects are willing to please you, the photographer/director, when you provide them with a comfortable, wide-open environment to work in. They prefer this to posing in a studio, which is a confined space filled with equipment. When children feel unencumbered, they reveal their true and usually charming personalities.

Kelly Michaelis, a freckled charmer who works in musical theater, wanted a straightforward headshot. This talented young performer has a smile that could melt ice. Because she is such a pro, directing Kelly to pose for a commercial headshot is like asking a dancer to dance. She was exceedingly easy to work with because she was accustomed to following directors' instructions. Here, I told Kelly to lean right into the camera on the metal reflector, which was propped up to support her. I wanted plenty of the flattering outdoor light on her face to give it extra freshness;

Kelly Michaelis

Katie Royce

I also wanted to fill the frame as much as I could with her sweet face and smile. Kelly's hair was swept back in a subtle ponytail. She wore a cream-colored, sleeveless pullover for this commercial shot. I decided against using any makeup; I thought that her freckles enhanced her appeal.

The composite featuring Katie Royce, another charmer, shows three different commercial shots. In the large picture, Katie is holding up her hair (left). Although this pose isn't usually seen in headshots, it works here. I backlit Katie's blonde hair just as I would have an adult's in order to give it highlights. Wearing a light-colored top with a Peter Pan collar, Katie looks as if she is really enjoying herself. I acted a little silly during the session to make her laugh. For example, I pretended to bump my head on the main light; when she laughed, I snapped the picture. Barbara, Katie's mother, and I kept the makeup minimal, adding just a touch of a medium-toned base and a splash of blush on the girl's cheeks. To give Katie's lips some color, I simply applied some cherry-flavored lip balm.

For another shot, I had Katie wear a deep-red jacket over her white top for contrast (top right). I aimed a fan at her hair here to add some movement. Katie's laugh is infectious. For the third shot of the composite, Barbara and I decided to style Katie's hair in pigtails with a pale blue ribbon (bottom right). After changing into a shirt with a quiet floral pattern, Katie showed the camera the sparkling vivaciousness that always helps her get work.

Although composites seem to be the favored marketing tool for very young models, such as six- and seven-year-olds, some agents are happy with a simple head-and-shoulders shot. As a result, you should do what the child's parent or manager wants. And because clients bring three or four outfits with them to the session, shooting a composite for them is no trouble at all.

NICE AND NATURAL

As mentioned earlier, hairstyling and makeup for any girl under the age of 10 should be minimal. If ever the natural look needs to be promoted, this is it. I suggest keeping the girl's hair, makeup, and wardrobe simple, medium-toned, and casual. And the darker the complexion, the lighter the clothes should be; you certainly don't want dark on dark. Of course, the look you create should be suited to your subject's personality. Remember, it is always a good idea to discuss your plans with your young client's parent(s) or guardian in advance.

The pictures in Cora Holden's composite show how effective this approach can be. In a formal shot, Cora wore a fancy but not too busy dress, and her hair was swept over to the right side of her face (right). Cora's large eyes pulled the whole look together. I then decided to have Cora wear a hat even though hats are usually taboo when it comes to headshots (left). The hat matched her sailor outfit perfectly and firmly established the casual feeling of this picture. As a result, Cora's composite is balanced.

Courtney Stone is another young subject whose terrific personality enabled me to try some hairstyles and costume choices that I ordinarily wouldn't consider. Nevertheless, I didn't overdo her makeup. After Courtney's mother helped me put just a bit of concealer under her eyes, I applied a thin layer of Cover Girl medium beige makeup. Courtney didn't need much base because she has a smooth complexion. Next, I used a very light hand while putting some blush just under her cheekbones; I wanted to give them a healthy, outdoors look. The terra-cotta shade that I selected is actually a deep rose that doesn't read too dark in a black-and-white image.

For one headshot, Courtney wore her hair back in a ponytail, a style that is usually acceptable for someone her age (left). Although her plaid top might seem a bit busy, she rose above it all. Courtney's other picture is more readily identifiable as a legit shot (right). Here, too, she dominated her clothing. Her striped shirt might seem rather bold for a professional headshot, but Courtney's concentrated eye contact enabled her to carry it. Although the woven pearl necktie was unusual, its very originality made the shot more interesting and attention-getting. For this quiet shot, I had Courtney wear her hair straight down, with just a slight curving in at the shoulders.

I backlit both shots so that Courtney's hair appeared to have plenty of body. I used a fan to effect a sense of movement. I kept the background light; I wanted just a tinge of gray. Light-toned backgrounds are a necessary ingredient for young subjects.

Cora Holden

Courtney Stone

ONE BOY, THREE LOOKS

Like everyone else interested in show business, boys need to have a variety of headshots taken. When they arrive at the session, they'll have several changes of clothes with them. The photographer's objective, then, is to capture three different looks. These are the commercial shot, which is essential for jobs that involve modeling clothes or posing with such products as a bicycle or a brand of cereal, and the legit or quiet shot, which is used for films and dramatic television shows. The third headshot, required for print work, falls in between the commercial and legit shots.

Sonny Tiedemann's three-shot composite reveals a spunky boy whose demeanor elicits the comment, "What a handsome boy." Naturally, while photographing Sonny, I decided to emphasize his big brown eyes. He worked very well with the camera and made better-than-average eye contact. At first he was a little unsure of my sense of humor, but he eventually accepted me as someone who was on his side. This is critical when you work with children. They must sense that you have their best interests at heart, and that you aren't arbitrarily imposing your will on them. Treating them with respect at all times will ultimately encourage them to trust you, as well as let you do what you have to do in order to get the best shot possible.

Sonny Tiedemann

Sonny's mother brought along three wardrobe changes. He wore a dark mock turtleneck for the commercial headshot (left). Although I prefer most of my clients to wear light-colored, open-collared shirts for this type of shot, I felt that this top suited Sonny's personality and didn't take away from his cute face or curly hair. All Sonny's mother and I had to do during the shoot was brush up his hair a bit now and then. Because Sonny has such a good complexion, we used little if any makeup. I chose a light background to create a sense of wide-open spaces.

Shooting Sonny's legit picture was a breeze (top right). His rapport with the camera is great because he almost burns a hole in the lens with his eyes. For this headshot, he wore a white, open-collared shirt under a leather vest. Although Sonny looks serious in his headshot, he doesn't appear morose or too thoughtful. As a photographer, you must be aware that permitting either of these countenances to surface in a legit headshot can be dangerous. As such, it is important for you to continually strive to keep your clients' emotions on an even keel. This is particularly true for children simply because most of the work that they're hired to do doesn't entail looking upset.

Sonny's third headshot on his composite shows off just enough of his sweater to qualify this picture as a print possibility (bottom right). His boxing stance is cute enough to be an attention-getter but still suggests that he wants to be a young actor.

CAPTURING A SPECIAL QUALITY

Whether I'm shooting in the studio or out in the park, I always try to give shots of boys a natural, rugged, outdoors look. Getting my subjects to appear laid-back and to make real eye contact with the camera is essential; to facilitate this, I keep parents or guardians at a safe distance emotionally. I want them on hand to help when needed and to make them part of the shoot, but I don't want them to attempt to direct the session. For example, when working outside, I ask parents to hold reflectors, keep a brush handy, and hold onto their children's clothing for potential last-minute changes. This keeps the adults busy and diverts their gaze from my subjects, so the children don't feel self-conscious.

To help boys feel comfortable in front of the camera, you can photograph them outside. Most boys prefer this arrangement to a studio session. All you have to do is bring a baseball glove, baseball, or football with you to serve as a prop. Of course, you don't have to include the prop in the headshot. When your subjects see the prop, they relax because they know that they're going to have a good time. Mention any kind of sports activity, and you've got a great conversation starter and icebreaker. Once you develop a rapport with your subject, the rest is easy.

Capturing Joshua Benton's special quality was simple. I've known Joshua and his parents for quite a few years, so he felt particularly comfortable with me. I also knew that he would follow directions well because he was a good listener. Miriam, his mother, was kind enough to act as my assistant during this on-location session. This handsome, young talent has a very expressive, giving personality, which is revealed in his big, brown eyes. I wanted Joshua's headshot to combine a studio feeling with the brilliance of a sunlit mood. To that end, I directed him to sit on the reading nook in the bay window. I then shifted his position so that the sun hit the back of his head. Next, I asked Miriam to hold the white reflective material a little above and just to the right of her son's face in order to add highlights to his eyes. Then I said something silly, and he smiled willingly. What also helped is the fact that Joshua likes to have his picture taken.

BAY WINDOW

WHITE
REFLECTOR

36

Joshua Benton

BRIGHT EYES

Brian Nolan's legit shot reveals his quiet intensity, but doesn't try too hard: Brian appears to be relaxed, and his slight smile prevents the image from being too heavy. I had Brian lean forward and rest his chin on his arms, and then I moved in for this striking closeup. He wore an open-collared, blue-plaid shirt. I backlit his blond hair to give it highlights, and I kept the background medium gray so that it wouldn't be too dark in the final images. This legit headshot is perfect for any kind of serious role; it indicates Brian's age, looks like him, and suggests that he has a serious side but that it doesn't dominate his persona.

Like Brian, Philip Ryan has big, bright eyes. His perky charm lights up a page. He seems to know that he has this quality, which gives him a sense of quiet self-assurance. Philip is the type of boy everyone has always made a fuss over, so he is somewhat used to the attention. As a result, he is terrific to work with. For this commercial headshot, Philip wore a green pullover sweater on top of a button-down white shirt. I kept the background light so that it would provide contrast with his brown hair, which I brushed down a bit to keep it neat. Like most other young boys, he didn't need to wear any makeup.

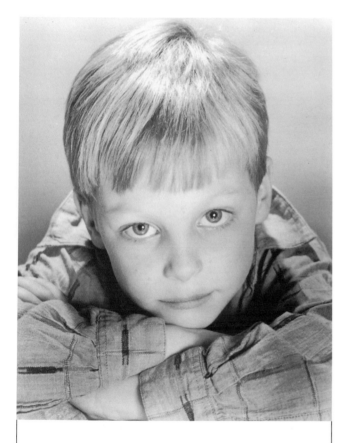

Brian Nolan

Philip Ryan

USING SIMPLE BACKGROUNDS OUTDOORS

When you shoot portraits of clients anywhere outdoors, it is particularly important that you stay away from overly fussy or busy backgrounds. You want the center of interest to be your clients' face, not the rosebush screaming for attention behind them. Be especially careful to avoid shooting in front of tree branches and clusters of leaves because they always distract and draw the focus away from the subject. Other backgrounds to avoid include lampposts, billboards, groups of people, overly ornate architecture, and cars whizzing by. Try instead to photograph your subjects against gray walls or open grass fields that rise up behind them and blur into neutral backgrounds.

I photographed six-year-old Michael Thum under a tree near his home. He'd been watching his favorite Saturday morning television show, so he was a bit distracted when I arrived. I waited patiently for him to come around, and his father was helpful in making him laugh. He stood directly behind me—which I don't mind when I work on location—and made funny faces.

For his commercial headshot, Michael wore a red-and-white striped shirt with a scoop neck. His hair was neither too long nor too short, and his complexion didn't call for any makeup. Naturally, I decided to feature Michael's terrific, large blue-green eyes. Here, he looked directly into the camera and burst into a wide-

Michael Thum

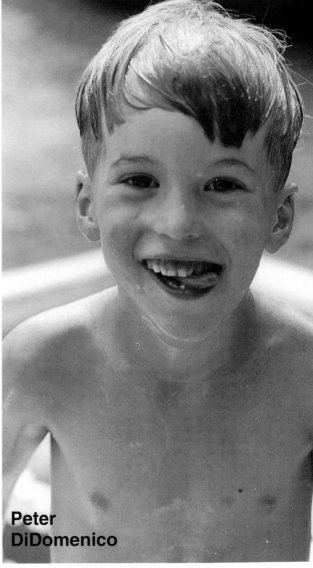

Peter DiDomenico

grinned smile that could sell anything from bubble gum, to ice cream, to Gap clothes for young boys.

The two commercial shots of vivacious, irrepressible Peter DiDomenico are good examples of what you can achieve when you photograph boys. In one picture, he'd just jumped out of the pool next to his house (left). This pose produced a refreshing stop-action image. Of course, his blond bangs were soaking wet, so neat hair was impossible. In his other shot, Peter is more subdued (below). Ordinarily, I try to avoid the use of hands in a headshot, but something quite special happened while I made this shot in the shaded light of the porch. Here, he wore a simple, dark-blue T-shirt and sat on an unobtrusive white wicker chair. Whatever his energy level, Peter presented himself as an affable boy, an ability that casting people love.

Peter DiDomenico

LIGHTING TECHNIQUES

Shooting outside is a big thrill for children. They know that they aren't going to be confined to the strictures of a studio space. If possible, I try to take my young clients outside for the first roll or two of film because working in wide-open spaces is so relaxing. It reminds them of going to the country, playing in the park, and running free in their grandparents' backyard.

Sometimes a gentle breeze blows the children's hair or clothes and adds a pleasant sense of motion to the pictures. And the fact that the shots are taken outdoors in and of itself implies action. This movement doesn't necessarily mean that your subjects must jump over fences or climb walls while you photograph them. You simply want to convey the idea that perhaps they were running or playing and then suddenly stopped and looked into the camera. Photographers are always attempting to capture this "stop action," this particular moment in time, and this special vibrancy. Another benefit of shooting on location is that the lighting is already present. All you have to do is take advantage of the flattering effects of bounced light or shaded light, or to shape the available light to your needs with reflectors.

The headshot of little Danielle Gaddy shows how successful a controlled-action picture shot outside can be. I made this charming shot of her as she leaned against a wall in a park. Danielle looks like she is up to something or is about to share a secret with you. Her big smile, casual hairstyle, delightful outfit, all of which is topped off with just a tad of makeup, combine for a headshot with lots of verve.

Blonde-haired Karen Christopher's headshot illustrates the outdoor-action concept perfectly, too. Here, she seems as if she'd been involved in some sporting event when someone came along and yelled hello, and she stopped and said "Hi!" back. This is a stolen moment of both excitement and communication, and Karen responded to the camera as it were a friend. The sun backlit her hair, and I had an assistant hold up a white illustration-board reflector about 3 feet from her face. The reflector was angled to Karen's left, so that it didn't hit her directly in the eyes.

You always want your subjects' eyes to be fully open, and shooting outside can cause some clients to squint. Blue-eyed individuals are often more sensitive to light than people with brown eyes. If you find that your subjects feel uncomfortable with the bright outdoor light, try photographing them in the shade where the illumination is softer. If, however, they still appear uneasy, take them back to your studio. Fortunately, most people can handle strong light. Despite her blue eyes, Karen dealt with the bright available light beautifully as I photographed her.

Danielle Gaddy

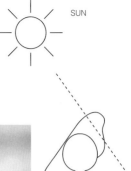

SUN

WHITE
REFLECTOR

105MM
PORTRAIT LENS
ON CAMERA

Karen Christopher

CHAPTER THREE
PHOTOGRAPHING TEENAGERS

The teenage years are a time of transition and new challenges on both a personal and professional level for aspiring actors and models. They have a number of physical, intellectual, and emotional changes to work through, too. Parents, teachers, agents, and managers ask them plenty of questions about their plans for their future. Headshot photographers should be aware of the conflicts going on in the heads of teenagers and, along with parents and agents, help shape the new image that they'll be presenting to the world around them.

As teenagers try to adapt to all of the new situations they find themselves in, their insecurities become more rampant than ever before. Some of the questions they ask themselves are: "How do I present myself?" and "What do people expect of me now?" Leaving childhood behind and moving into adolescence, they seek out the approval of others. Teenagers quickly learn that they can't rely on getting jobs or being accepted just because they are cute and little. They have to come to terms with their new appearance. Enabling teenage clients to get a firm grasp on how they want to come across in their headshots is, to a large extent, the job of the headshot photographer.

In this outdoor headshot, Jed Sexton looks happy and provides an example of the teenage personality at its best. Because he smiled directly at the camera, he comes across as sincere, honest, and relaxed. In contrast, plastered-on expressions are lifeless and dull. Jed's short hair suits his athletic appearance. To maintain his vibrant, natural look, I kept his tan makeup to a minimum. His dark leather jacket and black T-shirt contradict the established guidelines for a commercial shot, but sometimes exceptions to the rule lead to appealing pictures.

The bright illumination and Jed's exciting smile more than offset his dark outfit. I photographed him at one of my favorite New York City spots, the tunnel to the promenade in Riverside Park. I never need to use a reflector here because sunlight enters this open shaded space from above and then bounces off the ground in front of my subject, thereby acting like a reflector.

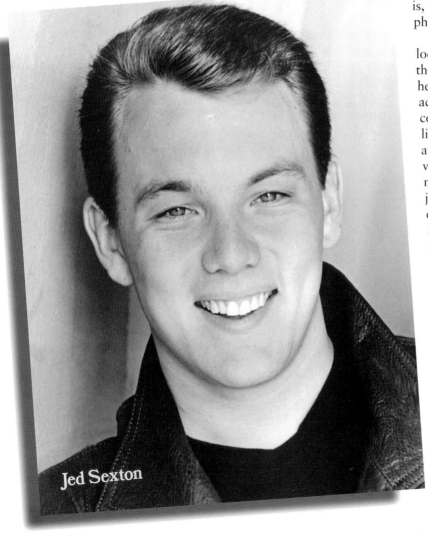

Jed Sexton

WARDROBE RECOMMENDATIONS

Clothing choices for teenagers can range from very casual to very dressy, and although most clients show up with five to seven outfits, I help them select the three or four changes suited to the different looks they want to achieve in the time allotted. It is best to start with a casual and relaxed-looking commercial/smiling headshot to ease into the shoot. I usually begin with a denim shirt or a light-colored top. Think of the outdoors, and stick with light pinks, blues, and yellows. For this shot, which often plays a big part in teenagers' careers, they want to look fresh and young, perhaps even younger than their actual age, but certainly no older. Naturally, this limits the use of makeup.

Teenage girls who are taking singing, dancing, and acting lessons to get work in the legitimate theater have several options. They can wear something on the dark side, such as a black bodysuit, for a somewhat serious look. But if your subject hopes to pursue musical comedy, she should wear light tones. Most aspiring soap-opera actresses lean toward dressy clothes.

The teenage subject who dreams of becoming a model can wear jeans for a casual look, a somewhat sophisticated blouse-and-skirt combination for a glamorous look, or a lycra-spandex outfit for an athletic look. Whatever approach the two of you decide to take, you must make sure that your young subject's clothes are appropriate for her age range.

For a quiet commercial shot, Shea Johnson wore the ever-popular Gap look, a denim jacket and white shirt. I directed her to lean into the camera, a pose that always infuses a headshot with extra energy and more intimate contact. In keeping with the minimal makeup and hairstyling recommendations for headshots of teenagers, I simply applied a good base to make Shea's face smooth and soft, slightly arched her eyebrows, and swept her hair back and away from her. Shea wore a medium shade of lipstick.

Teenage boys have a much simpler time preparing for their headshot session. Going for a casual, sporty look usually works best. Having T-shirts, button-down shirts, polo shirts, football jerseys, sweatshirts, V-neck sweaters, crew-neck sweaters, leather jackets, and windbreakers on hand provides me with a number of options. Sometimes I even suggest that a subject bring a jacket, dress shirt, and tie with him.

Michael Moon brought four wardrobe changes, ranging from casual to formal, to his shooting session. Together, we selected a sport jacket and a striped shirt. I told Michael not to wear a tie because I didn't want him to look like a young executive; an industrial portrait is rare for someone Michael's age. To cap off this appealing photograph, I directed my subject to smile wide and show off his beautiful teeth. The result is a successful commercial headshot.

Shea Johnson

Michael Moon

MAKEUP AND HAIRSTYLING RECOMMENDATIONS

Although hairstyling and makeup application aren't as much of a concern with teenagers, particularly males, as they are with adults, you must nevertheless give them some thought. The contour or shape of your subject's face is a primary consideration for both hair and makeup. If clients have long faces, they should try to avoid long hairstyles because these will only serve to exaggerate the shape of their face. In terms of makeup, you can minimize the effect of the elongation by sweeping blush into the front of the cheeks to cut the face in half. If, on the other hand, clients have round faces, they should wear their hair so that it cuts into or under the cheekbones. With these subjects, you can slim down the face by doing a little extra contouring under the cheekbones.

Keep in mind that blending is a critical part of makeup application. Achieving a natural look is paramount. You must make sure, for example, that lipsticks aren't too glossy and that blush colors are in the dark-pink and earth-tones range. Be aware that the contouring under the cheekbones and the shading of the nose (done only if it is somewhat round) should be softly blended, so that you preserve the freshness that is an integral aspect of a teenage girl's appeal.

Here, aspiring actress and model Kristen Green was having her long, blonde hair combed out before the session. The hairstylist brushed Kristen's hair back to give it extra body and bounce. I wanted her hair to look soft. During shooting sessions, however, I often tell teenage girls to throw their head forward, brush their hair up and away from the back of their neck, sit up again quickly, and then throw back their hair and sort of shake it out rapidly.

Another hairstyle option is to aim a fan at the subject's hair in order to blow it back and away from the face. Casting agents want to see people's faces, so they shouldn't be hidden under lots of curly hair. Don't get carried away if you decide to use one. Hairstyles for teenagers should be simple and unaffected. Any style that tries too hard and conceals or eliminates their bright-eyed image looks false.

When photographing African-American teenagers, I find that the hair's texture makes it easy to handle. And once again, I have several different styles to choose from, including a close-cropped cut or a fuller, combed-out look. For teenage girls from other ethnic groups, I confer with their mother and sometimes even their

agent for advice on what type of hairstyles they think are appropriate and flattering.

On occasion, teenage boys require some makeup. Use a good acne medication for skin breakouts, cover the blemishes with a medium base, and then brush a bronze/terra-cotta blush over the skin to create a just-back-from-Florida glow. Be sure not to make it too dark. Experiment until you find the right shades that work for your subjects. When it comes to their hair, teenage boys look best with a medium-length cut, not too long or too short, and a neat but not plastered down style.

WORKING WITH TEENAGE CLIENTS

Because teenagers are sensitive and impressionable, anything that a photographer can do to offset the individual's insecurities at the beginning of the shoot is welcome and appreciated. Make your young clients aware that their concerns are yours, and that you care what happens to them as much as they do. This will strengthen their sense of security during the preparation for the shoot and the shoot itself. Earlier discussions about the proper wardrobe, hair, and makeup will pay off during the photo session because you'll be firmly in control of what's happening and know what is expected. If seeing you take charge of all the details makes your subjects feel confident about the shoot, they might be able to give more of themselves to the camera. This in turn will make the session go smoothly.

When you work with teenagers, you must make sure that they don't come across as having an attitude. In its worst manifestation, an attitude is off-putting and intimidating. Posturing in the wrong way, making the shots look like the teenagers wants to be fashion models (when they aren't qualified to be), or simply looking like they are the best thing to happen to the acting profession since Meryl Streep and Dustin Hoffman, are turnoffs to casting directors. To prevent this problem from ruining a session, you must keep everything on an upbeat note. Remember, too, that teenagers form lasting impressions, so what you say can influence their behavior for years to come.

Heather McDonald's attitude makes for an appealing headshot. As a veteran of many commercials, she is a pleasure to work with. Her effervescent smile and beautiful teeth are exceptional. Because I wanted this portrait to look as if it had been shot outside, I told Heather to wear a light-toned T-shirt and a denim jacket. The result: a natural-looking headshot complete with a few freckles.

When you photograph teenagers, you must be sensitive to the fact that not every teenager who comes to your studio is going to look like Cindy Crawford or Marky Mark. You must be sensitive to any and all shortcomings with their complexion, hair, posture, size, and even the clothes that they bring to the shoot. You can always solve such problems. For example, the right makeup can conceal many complexion flaws, an extreme hairstyle can be reshaped, and a bizarre outfit can be toned down. Simply be diplomatic when you approach your subject and offer advice. Stress that the

Heather McDonald

final goal, getting great headshots, is worth the compromise, time, and trouble.

Finally, keep in mind that many older teenagers, especially boys, come to the studio on their own. Furthermore, many of them will have professional experience in the theater, commercials, soap operas, and/or films, so directing them throughout the session is easy. Of course, some older teenagers arrive with an agent, public-relations person, image consultant, and/or relative. In these situations, you must handle each additional person firmly but tactfully. Explain that they can assume a secondary role by assisting with wardrobe changes, for example, but that they can't direct the shoot.

MOTIVATING TEENAGERS

Inspiring teenagers to perform in front of the camera can be challenging. However, by giving teenage subjects a better sense of self, increasing their self-confidence, and helping them to believe that they're going to be (or to continue to be) very big in the entertainment business, you'll end up taking good headshots. And once they know that their wardrobe, hair, and makeup will be taken care of, they can relax and focus on their goal: to look great and get terrific new headshots that will get them even more work. When you work, you must act like a director. If you can clearly explain how you hope to capture your subjects on film in order to best represent them, both you and your subjects will be satisfied with the results.

While photographing Roger Mazzeo on location, I asked him about his career goals; knowing how he perceived himself allowed me to get two strong headshots. This background information also made encouraging him to reveal his personality relatively easy. Although his clothes are basically the same in the two shots, his expressions differ noticeably. For his commercial headshot, Roger wore a polo shirt and flashed a bright smile. Then for his legit shot, I told him to maintain his eye intensity but to appear thoughtful and serious. In this shot he wore a dark suede jacket, which he broke up with a white T-shirt. Thanks to Roger's willingness to listen to instructions, both shots work.

Roger Mazzeo

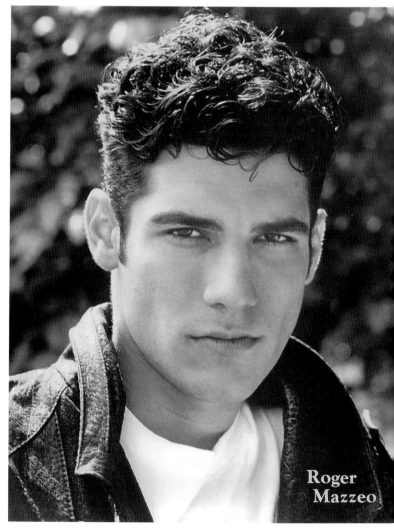

Roger Mazzeo

DEFINING AN INDIVIDUAL STYLE

When photographing teenagers, you need to think about the importance of making their headshots distinctive. One of the most effective ways to do this is to capitalize on each subject's uniqueness. Take advantage of the different ways your clients respond to the camera. Some teenagers feel quite comfortable posing, while others need to develop a professional attitude for the camera. I find that having them try the familiar but effective method of "talking to your friend the camera" works.

Jonathan Strait, who is in his late teens, related very well to the camera throughout his shooting session. He seems to jump out of the picture plane in an energetic but warm way. In fact, he projects charm, and his movie-star looks make him stand out from the competition. In order to get this shot, I needed to do more than merely tell Jonathan to smile; I had to motivate the young actor to look sincere while saying something meaningful to the camera. If you don't do this, your client's headshots will definitely look flat.

Jonathan
Strait

KEEP IT SIMPLE

When planning Elizabeth Phaire's session, she and I agreed that a slightly different approach would be best. For an unusual over-the-shoulders legit shot of this accomplished singer and actress, she styled her own hair. I limited Elizabeth's makeup to the essentials, mascara, blush, and base in the safe medium range of shades. Since Elizabeth projects a very natural glamour, I needed to add a small amount of gloss only to the center of the lower lip.

During her initial interview, Elizabeth told me she wanted a glamour mood for her headshot because she intended to submit it for auditions. To achieve this look, she wore a light, feminine, antique-lace top that framed her face and enhanced the overall composition beautifully without being distracting. I then decided to create a sort of MTV look for her shot. I wanted her curly blonde hair to appear that color in her black-and-white headshot, so I backlit it with a strong but filtered

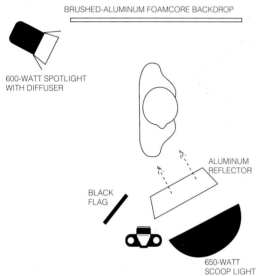

BRUSHED-ALUMINUM FOAMCORE BACKDROP

600-WATT SPOTLIGHT
WITH DIFFUSER

ALUMINUM
REFLECTOR

BLACK
FLAG

650-WATT
SCOOP LIGHT

Elizabeth
Phaire

600-watt spotlight. For the background, I selected a highly reflective brushed-aluminum backdrop that I'd rubbed with steel wool to soften the harsh bounce light. I kept the upper part of the background on the dark side so that it would contrast with and draw attention to Elizabeth's hair. Next, I illuminated her face with a 650-watt Lowell DP light, set to the "spot" position for a sharp, focused light; it functioned somewhat like a follow-spot used on performers in a nightclub. I positioned an aluminum reflector just below her shoulder line in order to bounce light into the shadows, make Elizabeth's skin luminous, and add sparkle to her eyes.

A simple approach utilizing an unusual angle seemed appropriate for Stephanie Stone, too. This charming teenager and I got along well when we worked together. I directed Stephanie to slightly tilt her head down. Her big, piercing blue eyes grab you and provide the primary focal point in the image. For this commercial headshot, Stephanie wore a severe black top and plain hoop earrings and sported a casual hairstyle that suited her personality.

Stephanie Stone

TRY A DIFFERENT FORMAT

In addition to the standard 8 x 10 format, some clients, acting schools, and agents request a three-quarter-length shot. Although this alternative larger format reveals more of the subject and enables viewers to get a better sense of the aspiring performer, this type of picture can lead to problems. If the subject's clothes dominate the three-quarter-length shot so that it becomes a fashion statement, casting people will think "model" not "actor" when they see it. As a result, it is absolutely critical that you choose your wardrobe for a large-format portrait carefully.

When planning Susan Rinaldo's session, I thought about ways to make her pictures look a little different from traditional headshots. She can project a great deal in a photograph without really trying thanks to her wonderful eyes. For this commercial headshot, Susan wore minimal makeup and a simple, white shirt, whose open collar she fingered. To effectively capture her vivacious spirit, I placed my key light just to her left side, and my reflector just to her right for shadow fill and for extra highlighting in Susan's big eyes. I backlit her hair softly with two 150-watt floods, one on either side of her head. I positioned a fan low in order to blow her hair back a little.

And when 13-year-old Christina Klymenko arrived at my studio with her mother, Olya, it was immediately clear that this teenager was a stunner. During the shoot, we tried several variations. Christina's wardrobe changes included this fitted T-shirt, a dark polo shirt, a white summer-knit sweater, and an olive sweater.

Toward the end of the shoot, I lent her a tan suede vest that I thought she would look great in. After taking the regular head-and-shoulders shots, I had Christina sit on a tall director's chair in order to shoot the three-quarter-length picture that her manager had specifically suggested.

Everything really clicked when Christina tried this new posture. I directed her to put her foot up on the seat and place her hand on her knee, a technique that I ordinarily use when shooting outdoors. This pose works here because it keeps the viewers' attention on Christina's ebullient personality rather than her clothes. I had the fan blowing on her, and I placed a reflective sky background behind her to augment the western theme. I used only a small amount of base, a smidgen of pink blush, and a bit of lipstick in the same deep-pink shade. This large-format shot is just as successful as her standard headshot.

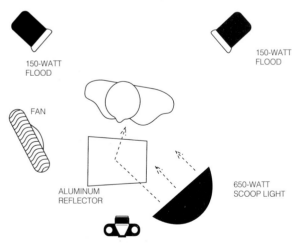

150-WATT
FLOOD

150-WATT
FLOOD

FAN

ALUMINUM
REFLECTOR

650-WATT
SCOOP LIGHT

Susan
Rinal•

Christina Klymenko

SHE'S UP FOR A COMMERCIAL

When clients come to me for what might be considered a high-fashion, "clotheshorse" type of composite, I always try to convince them that they should include a commercial shot, too. When petite Kristen Green arrived at my studio, I felt that her composite should lean as far as possible in the direction of the commercial-print field; this is modeling work that involves a commercial product rather than focuses strictly on fashion. She agreed with my assessment of her strong points, so we went ahead with my plan.

Kristen's commercial headshot has all the necessary elements: a great smile, an interesting pose, and fantastic personality projection (far right). This picture reveals how pretty she is and captures her vitality. Kristen has a warm, infectious smile, and I had her place her hand under her blonde hair to give a hint of high fashion. Although I spent a bit more time than usual applying Kristen's makeup because it is an interest of hers, it isn't overdone.

For the opposite side of Kristen's composite, I photographed her in three other poses that showed off her attributes in a most attractive way. The medium shot of her wearing a green-blue satin coat, for which I used the fan, adds a note of dash and glamour to the composite (left). For the full-length shot (center), she wore shorts and a floral-pattern halter top that accentuate her figure. Finally, I directed Kristen to tilt her head in a slightly different way for another closeup (right). No matter the pose or format, Kristen's eyes sparkle, and her smile dazzles.

Kristen Green

FINDING THE BEST ANGLE

When I first met Jeff Patten, I was impressed by the strong, athletic demeanor of this older teenager. During the initial interview, I discovered that he'd been to another photographer for headshots, but his agent felt that the shots didn't do him justice. They'd been taken from all the wrong angles, and he hadn't given enough to the camera to reveal anything particularly interesting about himself. For this casual headshot, he wore a light, zippered windbreaker over a white undershirt, and his hair was styled in a longish crew cut.

When preparing to photograph Jeff, my first step was to determine his best side. As I studied his face, I decided that his straight-on glance was so strong that I wouldn't need to use any special angles. With male subjects, it is frequently a good idea to shoot from an angle just a little lower than straight on in order to suggest height. Try to avoid shooting down on clients because this makes them seem smaller.

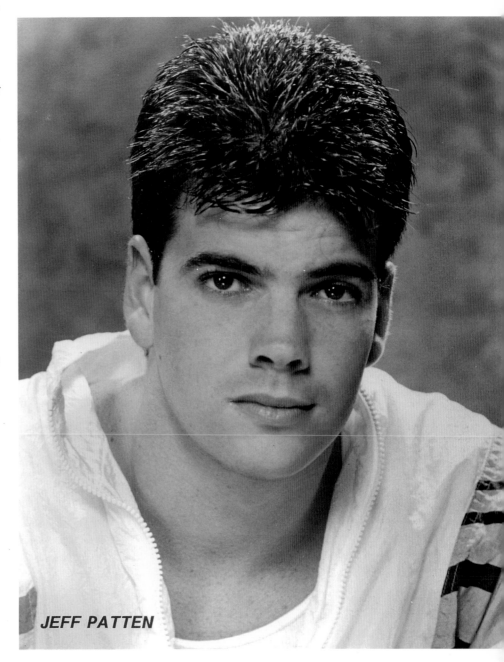

JEFF PATTEN

BOY ATHLETE

A popular headshot look for teenage boys is the athletic image, which 15-year-old David Klugh exemplifies. I thought that this type of shot would best reflect his personality. For his head-and-shoulders closeup, I used my trusty 105mm portrait lens (left). As I walked toward David (not zoomed in to him), he turned slightly to his right. I asked David's father to act as my assistant and hold up a white board, which bounced a small amount of reflected light onto David's face and give it a healthy glow. Since he was facing the light source, I was able to highlight his hair. The background is completely out of focus because I shot handheld at $f/8$ for 1/60 sec. Although this was David's first shooting session, he followed my direction easily.

Next, I decided to go with a longer shot (right). To keep this legit headshot looking cool and casual, I directed David to hold a football and lean against a tree in his front yard. If you shoot outdoors and want to include trees in your pictures, you have to make sure that they don't take up too much room visually and dominate the image. Here, the tree fills up less than a tenth of the picture area and is still recognizable. Composing judiciously before you shoot a scene prevents foregrounds and backgrounds from becoming distractions and deflecting attention away from the focal point of the picture, your subject.

Keep in mind that backdrops used in the studio can be just as problematic. If mural photographs or paintings of woods, waterfalls, or other landscape scenes are done badly, they can look fake. One way to keep them looking realistic is to place them back far enough so that they are out of focus.

David Klugh

STAR QUALITY

Some teen subjects have "star" written all over them. Teenager Stephan Roy is one of these people. An actor, model, and professional saxophone player with brown eyes and excellent teeth, he was also a pleasure to work with. Stephan has such a great sense of his own image that shooting various looks for his composite was easy.

For the all-important smiling shot, Stephan wore a deep-blue silk shirt, which was open at the collar (left). His eye contact in this commercial shot is special; I think that in this picture, he truly shows excitement in the eyes, which agents want to see. Stephan likes—and looks good with—the wet look, so I simply brushed his hair back a bit for this shot. I then decided to go with an entirely different look for Stephan; I wanted to portray him as a serious actor as well (right). In this shot, he wore a maroon jacket over a white T-shirt. Both of these headshots clearly show that this handsome teenager has star quality.

STEPHAN ROY

LIGHTING TECHNIQUES

The last but by no means the least step in the headshot process is coming up with an effective lighting setup for your subject. You must give some careful thought to a well-placed main light, a supplemental reflector just under the clients' face, a properly positioned backlight or hairlight, and an unobtrusive background. This backdrop should be on the dark side for blond-haired subjects—for example, deep gray—and on the light side—perhaps charcoal gray—for dark-haired individuals. A background should rarely be black.

Lighting designs for teenagers should reinforce their youthfulness. You should illuminate their faces well in order to give their skin a kind of inner glow. If a poor complexion is obvious, you can play it down with a good liquid-base coverup topped with a matte pressed powder and tannish blush. Don't use too much sidelighting; it serves only to exaggerate blemishes.

When planning a lighting setup, you also need to think about illuminating the hair from behind to bring out its highlights. Headshots of teenagers don't require dim or dark lighting, even if the client's picture will be submitted for a horror movie. Professional headshots on both coasts are slightly understated, not overly dramatic. They aren't moody and dismal. They should reflect your subjects' in-control emotions and temperament, and send out this positive message: "This is me at my best. Hi!"

Casting agents for television series, pilots, and films want actors to look like their headshot when they walk into the casting office. As a result, excessive makeup, fussy hairstyles, wild clothes, and distracting lighting techniques defeat the purpose. The features of teenage actors cry out to be seen, not hidden by outrageous hair, makeup, and/or clothes, or poor lighting.

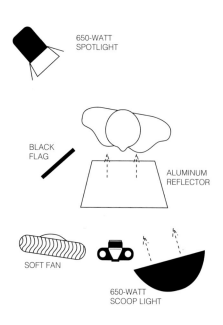

650-WATT SPOTLIGHT

BLACK FLAG

ALUMINUM REFLECTOR

SOFT FAN

650-WATT SCOOP LIGHT

Leila Bingl

When aspiring actress Leila Bingley and her parents came to my studio, we agreed that a straightforward approach would work best for her legit headshot. Sticking to basics, she wore a denim jacket for this picture. Since Leila has a stunning face, her mother and I left it pretty much alone on the day of the session. Perhaps her most compelling feature is her intelligence, which is reflected in her sincere eyes. The three of us established an easy rapport that day, which made the shoot go smoothly. This was partially responsible for Leila's spirit and is reflected in this compelling headshot of an eager, young actress.

Since Leila has such a striking face, I was able to move my main light in rather close and then opened up by half a stop. Wanting to capture a spontaneous, fresh, apple-pie image of Leila, I achieved strong frontlighting with my 650-watt flood. To further increase the illumination, I placed my trusty reflector just under the camera level so that it was between the camera and my subject.

Robin Myles also has a memorable face. At age 13, her bone structure is already phenomenal. During her last shoot with me, we decided to do a composite to showcase her blossoming beauty. For her three-quarter-length shot, Robin wore jeans and a polo shirt (left). I had her sit on one of my rectangular stands, and she seems to be in control of the whole situation. This large-format shot also emphasizes her naturally curly blonde hair that falls just below her shoulders. The makeup application was low-key because I wanted to keep her sweet, youthful appearance.

In her commercial shot, Robin wore a red tennis sweater that gave her a sporty look (top right). I put a low fan on her hair, blowing it back just a bit. This gave the shot a sense of outdoor movement and dash. Finally, I took a legit shot of Robin (bottom right). This photograph, for which she put on a white tank top, has a straightforward, "let's be friends" feeling. As this composite shows, a girl like Robin could wear almost anything and make it look terrific.

Robin Myles

PHOTOGRAPHING TWENTYSOMETHING WOMEN

As a headshot photographer, you must be able to adapt to variations in appearances when you work with clients belonging to different age groups. You have to make subjects look great in their portraits no matter what the calendar says. For example, as teenage girls move into their twenties, they obviously develop a more mature look. In addition, their bone structure becomes more pronounced; their attitude, more sophisticated; and their wardrobe, makeup, and hairstyles, more personalized.

Sensitive photographers are keenly aware of these individual differences. Furthermore, at this point in a young woman's life, potential stardom seems rather close at hand. As a result, the conversations you have with your twentysomething clients during both the initial interview and the shooting session itself consist of more give and take than they do when you work with children. This straightforward, positive attitude is as important to shooting great headshots as your female subjects' newfound beauty is.

When Clarissa D. Newby and I first met, she told me that she wanted a sophisticated headshot, but not so chic that it would make her look a few years older than she actually is. A professional singer and actress with an impressive resumé,

Clarissa chose an outfit that reflects her glamorous performer image. The dress's black-velvet straps embrace her shoulders, and her drop earrings frame her face beautifully. I used just enough mascara to emphasize her eyes; too much eye makeup can age a subject. I backlit Clarissa's hair, which was styled in a French twist, and aimed a 650-watt spotlight at her face to establish a performance mood.

Clarissa D. Newby

WARDROBE RECOMMENDATIONS

With a new, sophisticated approach to wardrobe, young actresses look quite attractive. Naturally, if the clothes your subject wears are suited to her individual look and persona, she'll feel good about herself and more at ease in front of the camera. To achieve this level of comfort, you and your client must address the wardrobe question with great care before the shoot; the two of you must thoroughly discuss the various outfits she'll bring to the session in terms of their color, texture, tailoring, and style.

Suppose, for example, that you scheduled an appointment for 2 o'clock on a Wednesday afternoon. After you exchange an affable greeting at the door to your studio, you show the client to the dressing room. The next step is to lay out or hang up her clothes in the order in which they'll be used. Proper accessories are also selected for each wardrobe change. Ordinarily, I adhere to the following sequence of shots.

First, I do the commercial headshot. Pastel shades are perfect choices for women in the twentysomething age range, and blouses and shirts with V-necks are preferred. Remember, the goal here is to capture a fresh, relaxed, smiling look that "goes straight into the camera."

The second scheduled picture is the legit shot. This headshot is usually taken for the theater, although it can overlap into soap operas and films. Quieter than the commercial headshot, the legit shot is sincere and calls for the subject to make strong eye contact with the camera. I then move on to the industrial shot. Here, your clients dress as if they work on Wall Street or at a huge corporation, such as IBM. The goal is the young executive look, so a light-toned blouse and a darker jacket are appropriate. The client's hair is swept back a bit, and her makeup is simple.

Finally, I shoot the glamour headshot, which is needed for soap-opera, film, and print work. This shot calls for sex appeal. Think Hollywood, Las Vegas, or Broadway, and go all out. Your client's clothes should be more extravagant and expensive than they are for the other three types of headshots. Feel free to have fun with sequins, satins, and silks. You can also apply makeup with a somewhat heavier hand based on individual taste.

During Sherri Johnson's session, she wore two very different outfits. For her legit shot, she chose an open-collared denim shirt for a casual look (right). The tilt of her head and her serious countenance give this photograph a compelling power. Sherri then changed into a flattering black-sequin gown for her glamour headshot (left). To take advantage of the glittering sequins, I used a spotlight as my main light; I also needed a 150-watt hairlight to separate my subject from the dark background. No reflector was required. I wanted this to be special, so I used a black-silk oriental screen embroidered with gold-thread designs.

Sherri Johnson

MAKEUP APPLICATION AND HAIRSTYLING

Although hair and makeup are critical to the outcome of a young woman's headshot, you'll find that most subjects in this group have a very good idea of what works for them. This is immediately apparent during the first interview when you discuss an actor's complexion, as well as the correct base and blush. Often, clients are already wearing what is most becoming to them, so you simply have to increase the makeup a bit during the shoot to compensate for the studio lights. You can determine the intensity of the makeup either in the dressing room or on the set itself to take into account the effect of the key light.

On occasion, however, clients want to have their hair and makeup done before arriving for the session. They have several options. Your subjects can do their hair and makeup themselves, have this done by a makeup artist they've worked with before, go to the cosmetic counter of any large department store and have it done gratis or with a nominal purchase, or bring their own hairstylist/makeup artist with them to the shoot. If a client so desires, I can recommend a makeup artist/hairstylist. Any of these approaches is fine.

But you must make it clear to your clients that you insist on acting as the final arbiter of the makeup requirements for working under the lights, and for making the transitions between the different types of headshots. For example, you might decide to first do the commercial shot, which calls for light makeup and simple hairstyles, followed by the glamour shot, which is characterized by deeper shades of lipstick, more contouring, and darker mascara. You must see how these makeup applications play under the lights and make any necessary changes. The most common adjustments involve contouring with blush under the cheekbones.

Makeup application and hairstyling for twentysomething women call for precision. For example, when makeup artists use eyeliner, they are careful to keep it from going too black and harsh because an excess amount can impart a cheap look. They also add a touch of concealer or lightener under the client's eyes, where everyone tends to go a little dark there. Professionals also know that brushing the eyebrows with a special brush improves their appearance, and that an eyebrow pencil fills in any weak areas. Skilled artists also know that putting a soft gloss on the lips add a tad more life to them.

Although styling hair should be a simple procedure, most people fuss more over their hair than they do their makeup. After all, their hair is their proverbial crowning glory, so they make sure that it is just right. If clients are unhappy at all when their shots are printed, 90 percent of the complaints are in reference to the hair.

Here, makeup artist/hairstylist Krista Lorn puts the finishing touches on client Denise Simone's hair and makeup. Since Denise was wearing pearl earrings and a brushed-silk blouse, the desired effect was a stunning glamour presentation. Most women know what looks best on them and want to stick with it, but some are open to suggestions and may even want to try a new look. In these situations, the photographer may have some ideas or the professional hairstylist can make some suggestions. Like makeup application, hairstyling can be done before a client arrives for her session, either by herself or by her own stylist.

I always keep a set of hot rollers in the dressing room of my studio and a curling iron on hand in case they're needed for a shoot. Once a subject's hair is appropriately set and styled, I decide whether or not I need to use some soft backlighting on it to give it more body and life. Of course, the key light also adds attractive highlights to hair. I dislike shots that make hair look like a dark, flat silhouette. No matter what the color, blonde, red, brunette, or black, you should pay special attention to your subjects' hair so that it fits their individual personality and enhances the overall image they want to promote.

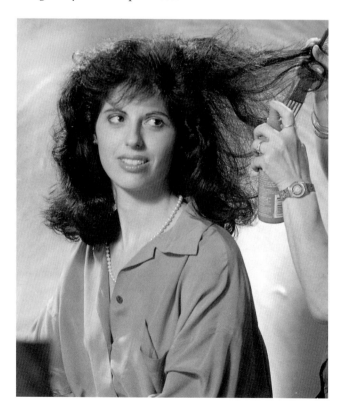

FAN-TASTIC EFFECTS

You can use a fan to give a subject's hair some lift as well as to make it seem alive as it gently blows the hair back and away from the face. During the course of the session, you can use a fan frequently but not continuously. The fan effect is always appropriate for the glamour headshot, sometimes suitable for the commercial shot, rarely acceptable for the legit shot (only when musical comedy is the venue), and never appropriate for the staid industrial shot. Exactly when and how you use the fan is up to you. Even when I decide not to utilize a fan for my work, I usually have it blowing gently on the faces of most clients during the entire shoot to keep them cool, refreshed, and relaxed. You should simply keep it in the back of your mind as another way to invigorate your photographs of your female clients.

For this headshot of Paige Pickens, I thought that using a fan would provide an extra bit of movement and vitality to the shot. This young woman has luxurious red hair, which is sometimes difficult to illuminate. To distinguish red hair from brunette hair, I saturate it with light. Here, I used a 650-watt lamp to produce plenty of modulated backlighting. Then I placed my key light off to Paige's right and the reflector just under her chin. The result is stunning.

Paige wore a great tuxedo top, which is a little out of the ordinary for a headshot. To break up the white tone, I directed her to place her hand on the shirt collar. Notice that her slim hand doesn't interfere with her face. Paige's makeup is more defined than that of some of my other twentysomething clients, but this is her look. The final touch was a pair of seed-pearl earrings.

Paige Pickens

THE INGENUE

One of the most popular looks for women in the twentysomething age bracket is that of the ingenue. The goal of this approach is to record your subjects' fresh beauty and bright personality. Remember, these clients are young, so capitalize on their appealing youthfulness. For example, Marni (the name she uses professionally) comes across as honest and vital. Because I didn't want to draw attention away from her sweet face, I had her hair brushed back and applied her makeup judiciously. In keeping with this objective, Marni wore a simple scoop-neck sweater and tiny earrings. She made fantastic eye contact with the camera. That extra sparkle in her eyes is the result of a strong key light, supplemented by the reflector balance. Obviously, Marni is a young rising star who is full of enthusiasm and energy.

Kathryn Riedman's commercial headshot is captivating, too. She has the type of personality that lights up any room she walks into. Her big smile is infectious. Because she wore a light-toned plaid jacket over a light-blue blouse, this commercial shot could also be used as an industrial headshot.

Photographing this aspiring actress in my studio, I backlit her light-blonde hair to give it lively highlights, and I was careful not to cause any hot spots. I aimed my key light, a 650-watt scoop light, straight at Kathryn and just below the standard 45-degree angle; the reflector was held directly under her chin. Keep in mind that depending on the shape and length of your subject's nose, you can lower or raise the key light to the right level in order to eliminate the dark shadow that might form under the nose.

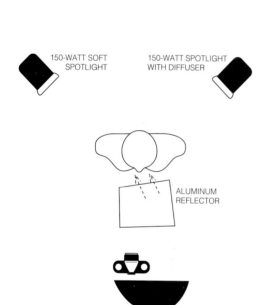

150-WATT SOFT SPOTLIGHT

150-WATT SPOTLIGHT WITH DIFFUSER

ALUMINUM REFLECTOR

650-WATT SCOOP LIGHT WITH DIFFUSER

Kathryn Riedman

MARNI

LETTING THE PERFORMER EMERGE

The legit headshot, which is somewhat more contemplative and controlled than the energetic commercial shot, covers performers for basic dramatic work for the theater. Such nonmusicals include comedies, tragedies, and in-between melodramas. In order to provide clients with an effective legit shot for this purpose, you need to capture their quiet side.

Maria Bellow's headshot suggests that she can play difficult parts by such masters of drama as Tennessee Williams, Henrik Ibsen, Anton Chekhov, and Arthur Miller. She chose a dark jacket and a basic blunt hairstyle for this serious shot. Maria's gaze is so intense in this picture that it seems to burn off the page. She has an amazing ability to project feelings; as a result, this legit headshot is a winner.

Other actresses might want to emphasize a different quality. For example, Raquel Bianca can achieve intense eye-to-eye contact with a single glance because she is so talented at playing to the camera. The chemistry she can generate when working in a relaxed atmosphere and doing what she does best is amazing. The movie-lighting setup I arranged enhanced Raquel's simmering sex appeal. I used a gently blowing fan on her wavy, brunette hair to enhance its tousled appearance. Her tailored gray jacket puts the finishing touch on this striking legit headshot.

The real challenge for headshot photographers is to capture their clients' changes in mood, those subtle switches from one emotional state to another that can occur spontaneously—and unexpectedly. Photographers also must find something special inside that sets one subject apart from everyone else. Wardrobe, hair, and makeup are merely accoutrements; they don't constitute your clients' essential core.

Maria Bellow

Raquel Bianca

A WINNING SMILE

All aspiring performers hoping to succeed in the entertainment field—actors, singers, musicians, and comics—must have a great commercial shot that showcases their smile. They need to show managers and casting agents that they are upbeat and enthusiastic about their chosen profession. If their commercial headshot doesn't convey these qualities, they'll never be considered for a job.

For Kim D'Armond's smiling headshot, she wore a textured, cream-colored jacket over a raspberry scoop-neck top. Her freedom of expression and young freshness combine perfectly to illustrate the ideal commercial shot for a twentysomething woman. I used a deeper background to bring out Kim's honey-colored hair. Her eyelashes are incredibly long and serve to frame her sparkling blue eyes.

Kim D'Armond

THE HOLLYWOOD LOOK

If you want to create an updated version of a 1930s or 1940s glamour shot of Lana Turner or Rita Hayworth, Rebecca Bowman's headshot can serve as an inspiration. She wore a sleeveless, pale-chiffon gown and smiled with a provocative innocence. I placed a 350-watt backlight, with a screen and plastic diffuser, about 2 feet above and behind her head to make her red hair stand out against the dark-gray background. Next, I positioned a 650-watt spotlight at a 45-degree angle to Rebecca's face at a distance of 5 feet, and a 150-watt hair light about 2 feet above and to the left of her head for fill. I also used an aluminum reflector on a 3-foot-high stand positioned just below her chin and about 3 feet in front of her. This kept her gray eyes from looking darker than they actually are. The result is right out of old Hollywood.

Denise Simone's headshot provides another example of the Hollywood glamour look. I had her lean in toward the camera to achieve a provocative look. I used a diffused 600-watt backlight to produce a strong contrast between her dark hair and her complexion. To bring out Denise's fine bone structure, I applied a deep terra-cotta blush to her cheekbones and positioned the key light to her right for a spotlight effect that revealed her great bone structure and shaded her nose. This lamp highlighted her large brown eyes as well. Next, I placed an aluminum reflector below her hand and tilted it to her left side to fill in the shaded areas. Finally, I added a very soft hair light.

Denise wore an off-the-shoulder, scoop-neck top that I decided to crop out. Drop crystal earrings completed the glamour look. As I photographed her, she held her hair up with her right hand.

Remember, although you may be doing the same type of shot, you must always be aware of your clients' unique features and try to capture them on film. Don't grow careless and complacent and do what I call assembly-line work, which is done in passport-photography "studios." Although this is an extreme situation, forewarned is still forearmed, especially when those arms are full of cameras about to photograph real, live human beings. Keep in mind that it isn't the glamorous trappings you're photographing, but the very special, very fragile psyche of an actor or executive. The actors themselves will give you what you need for a glamour shot. The striking results will come from their talent, not feather boas.

Rebecca Bowman

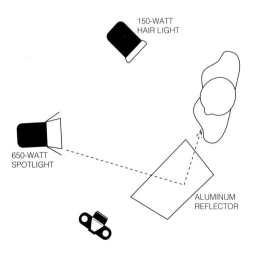

150-WATT HAIR LIGHT

650-WATT SPOTLIGHT

ALUMINUM REFLECTOR

350-WATT BACKLIGHT WITH DIFFUSER

DENISE SIMONE

NATURAL GLAMOUR

The many books, videotapes, and magazine articles on how to photograph glamour shots often call for lots of feathers, sequins, soft focus, few clothes, and little personality projection. As far as headshots are concerned, however, if an aspiring actor submitted a picture filled with those elements to a legitimate casting agency, the staff members would view the shot as a cheap, pushy, blatant image and dismiss it out of hand. Acting is acting; it isn't an exercise in the application of heavy makeup and the use of industrial-strength starburst filters. For the acting profession, glamour is in the restrained projection of a self-confident allure. After all, true glamour comes from within.

Television actress Terri Garber's headshot illustrates how engaging real glamour can be. Here, her appeal comes from her unassuming demeanor. Her potential is quite evident in her eyes, her sweet face, and graceful hand gesture. Terri has "it," but she isn't flaunting it.

Karen McArn is a soap-opera actress, which her photograph reveals. In this glamour headshot, she looks very upscale and classy. It shows off her beautiful face in a soft way. The picture also has a natural quality that speaks volumes about Karen without shouting about her. She wore a light-blue, textured-silk blouse. Although her hair is full, her face is readily visible. I used only enough makeup to create an impression; I certainly didn't have to contour her prominent cheekbones too much.

Karen McArn

Terri Garber

PERSONALITY FIRST, FASHION SECOND

A new trend in professional headshots is the acceptance of the fashion/figure portrait. Some agents and acting schools seem quite enthusiastic about and interested in this alternative. However, as a headshot photographer, you shouldn't let the subjects' figures dominate these three-quarter-length shots. Their purpose isn't to show off the clothes that your subjects are wearing, but to reveal something about them. As you shoot, remember that the focus here is people, not wardrobe. Keep in mind, too, that if you can't decide whether to go with the three-quarter-length shot or the traditional headshot, which is still preferred by most clients, you can always put both on an 8 x 10 composite.

Your clients' personalities must come across loud and clear in their large-format photographs, otherwise these shots are self-defeating. You must also take great care to have the subject appear to be at ease and the pose to look natural, never arch or excessively attitudinal. When working with Yung Moon, I photographed her from a slightly lower angle to capture just a hint of attitude. Because of her regal reserve, she exudes quiet sophistication. Yung looks intriguing here, not intimidating. For this shot, she wore a silk paisley blouse over a black top. Her smart

Keeley
Stanley

hairstyle suits the shape of her face perfectly, and her dangling earrings set off her marvelous bone structure. I placed the main light just to the right of her head in order to emphasize her facial contours.

Yung is an aspiring actress, and she and I felt that this photograph would tell casting people that this is her style for dramatic roles. The clothes and accessories are great, but they don't overpower her. Of course, I also took some smiling shots of Yung wearing a white suit, but I prefer this show stopper. This image has an arresting quality that works for me.

I made Keeley Stanley's three-quarter-length shot outdoors. I instructed her to practically face directly into the sun as I photographed her. This was an unusual request; I ordinarily tell subjects to turn away from the sun. But that day the sky was overcast, and the sun wasn't extremely harsh on Keeley's eyes and complexion. In fact, although her letter jacket looks great over her plaid Pendleton shirt, her pose is what makes this shot succeed. Her blonde hair and light-blue eyes add to her charm.

Yung
Moon

STRIKE A POSE

Michelle Buchner is one of the most attractive dancers I've ever photographed, and I wanted her to look like a ballet dancer in her pictures. For this legit headshot, she wore a light-toned leotard top to help create the effect I was after. But what makes this shot work so well is Michelle's pose. Her torso is turned away from the camera, thereby causing her to turn her head and neck so that she faces the camera. This position, along with the slight tilt of her head, leads to direct eye contact.

Michelle inspired me so that I used a new background. I wanted something soft and theatrical that wouldn't attract attention to itself yet would enhance Michelle's sophistication. When I came across a gauze canopy intended to be hung over a bed, I knew that I'd found what I was looking for. I brought the canopy to my studio, hung it from the ceiling, and then illuminated it different ways. By backlighting it with a 150-watt soft

spot, I achieved the effect I wanted. In Michelle's headshots, the spot shines through two layers of what looks like mosquito netting, and appears soft and glowing. This, in turn, establishes the ballet/theatrical setting and offsets Michelle's pose. Considering alternatives to the customary flat, painted backgrounds can enable you to give clients innovative headshots.

Maribelle Suarez is another pretty and talented singer/dancer with an extraordinary ability to relate to the camera. Without this, a client's headshots are lackluster and uninteresting. She also knows how to pose so that she capitalizes on her sex appeal, but doesn't look provocative. In this commercial shot, the slight turn of Maribelle's head and neck are a bit unusual; this is a subtle variation of the straight-on pose and makes viewers take notice of her bright, inviting smile.

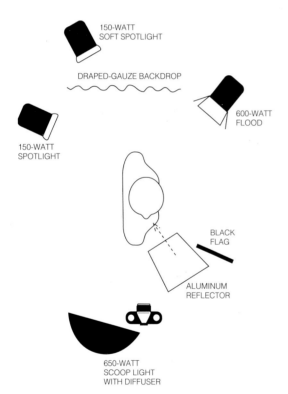

150-WATT
SOFT SPOTLIGHT

DRAPED-GAUZE BACKDROP

600-WATT
FLOOD

150-WATT
SPOTLIGHT

BLACK
FLAG

ALUMINUM
REFLECTOR

650-WATT
SCOOP LIGHT
WITH DIFFUSER

Michelle Buchner

Maribelle Suarez

CARNEGIE HALL, HERE I COME

Photographing singers can be a great deal of fun. Simply tell them to bring a tape of their songs to the session, and listen to the music as you work together. This is the only motivation your subjects will need to get on with the shoot. They're continually working on lyrics and music for new songs, practicing with groups and bands, and performing wherever they can just so that they can be heard. Singers are always bubbling over with enthusiasm for their work, too, so capturing their excitement during a session is relatively easy for you.

Opera singer Allison Foster brought several different and interesting gowns to her shoot. I wanted to shoot an inspired image of her that would show Allison off to her best advantage. The first three gowns photographed well, but it wasn't until she pulled a piece of soft, gray fabric out of her suitcase that I knew I could create just the right look for her. I simply had Allison wrap the cloth around her shoulders, and everything fell into place. This haute-couture glamour, complimented by her white-jade earrings, neatly cut hair, and arresting eyes, allows Allison's inner loveliness to come through.

Lucille DeCristofaro, a cast member of Broadway's *Les Misérables*, wore a black-lace gown with a scoop neckline for her legit headshot. Her deep-auburn, shoulder-length hair is one of this attractive woman's best features. As usual, I wanted to highlight her hair to emphasize its sleek shape, so I backlit it with two 150-watt fresnels, one on either side of her head. While applying her makeup, I made sure that I emphasized her arched eyebrows to bring out her luminous eyes. Using a deep terra-cotta blush, I shaded softly just above her cheekbones to widen her eyes somewhat. (I never use dark-brown eye shadow when shooting in black and white because they produce a harsh look; I prefer to stay with deep-pink shades, which are softer and more flattering.) Lucille's cool self-assurance and quiet strength are integral parts of her personality, both of which are captured in this headshot.

Allison Foster

Lucille DeCristofaro

MAKE 'EM LAUGH

Vivacious Marla Schultz, an up-and-coming comedy star, wore an army-officer jacket for her headshot. Throughout most of the shoot, I just let her be herself. I also had her perform a little and told her to pretend that the camera was her audience; this is often a good strategy when you work with people who perform. Letting them do a bit of their material helps them feel comfortable and enables you to get a better sense of their potential. Here, Marla's bright eyes and big smile make her look enthusiastic and eager to get on stage.

Marie Ottavia's composite shows off the versatility of this character actress, who is also a comic and a cabaret singer. After shooting traditional headshots of Marie, she and I agreed that experimenting a bit might lead to successful pictures. Revealing her humorous side, she posed as a happy photojournalist on safari (left), a harried office worker (top right), and a chef who is very impressed with a reluctant lobster (bottom right). Although I don't ordinarily use a lot of props, their inclusion demonstrates how much fun you can have with them, as well as what you can do with a little imagination. A composite like this is quite popular on the West Coast.

Marla Schultz

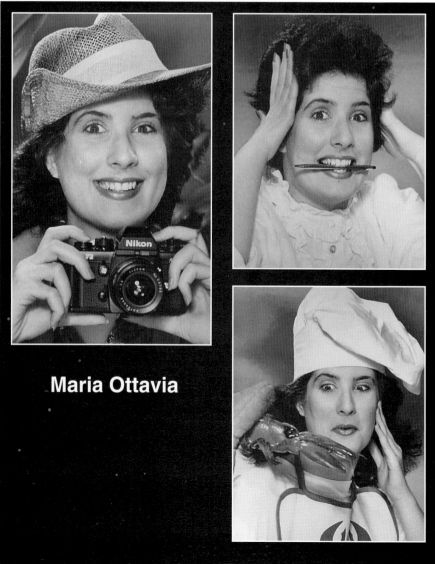

Maria Ottavia

74

THE MULTITALENTED PERFORMER

Songa Laster's composite illustrates her many talents, which include singing and acting. She also appears in commercials. I decided to photograph her in a variety of poses to reflect this attractive, ebullient performer's wide-ranging skills. Songa's large commercial headshot is featured on her composite; her smaller legit and industrial headshots, which make up the rest of the composite, balance it nicely. Have fun when you begin to design a client's composite. You might be dealing with five or six 8 × 10 glossies at a time, so you should play around with these enlargements in order to see which arrangement of shots has the most powerful graphic impact.

For her commercial headshot, Songa wore a denim shirt with the collar raised a bit to accentuate her neck and to add flair (left). Of course, you can leave a shirt collar flat or simply lift it a little just behind the neck. Don't raise the collar at all when photographing subjects with short necks. Doing so will only call more attention to this feature. Songa changed into a soft-blue chiffon gown for her legit shot (top right). Her hair was curled more to make her look glamorous. I emphasized her makeup somewhat, but her hairstyle and dress are the elements that make this shot a standout. Finally, the industrial shot depicts a somewhat severe Songa, yet her eyes and quiet smile prevent viewers from taking her too seriously (bottom right). Songa and the hairstylist decided to arrange her hair more on top of her head to suggest a certain reserve.

I used a soft-cloud background for Songa's commercial shot, and a softly mottled background for both the legit and the industrial shots. I was careful to plan the lighting designs in such a way that I was able to illuminate the backdrops enough to give them a life of their own, but not to draw too much attention to them. I love a feeling of space in any portrait.

Songa Laster

LIGHTING TECHNIQUES

During my initial meeting with Stella Pierce, I liked her immediately. First, she did her own makeup superbly. Second, she brought clothes that she knew were right for her. And perhaps most important, she had a fantastic ability to take direction. To create this dynamic headshot, I aimed the key light pretty much straight at my subject. Then I backlit her luxurious hair with a strong 650-watt flood and used a 150-watt rimlight on her right side. As a result of the lighting setup, Stella was illuminated very strongly from three different angles, front, back, and side. The magic reflector was positioned just below the bottom of frame.

My first meeting with Penny Balfour was equally enlightening. I discovered that she wanted a straightforward headshot photographed outdoors in only available light. She hoped to avoid artificial, overly airbrushed studio shots because they look so stiff. For this legit shot, I kept the makeup understated to create an outdoor feeling. Penny's hair, which was just a bit shorter than shoulder length with light bangs, was brushed away from the face. Her eye contact is direct and believable. The slightest of friendly smiles keeps the shot from being too serious.

Since I was shooting on a sunny June day around 3 o'clock in the afternoon, I knew that Penny's hair would be backlit by the sun's rays at approximately a 45-degree angle. This produces only a small triangular shadow under the subject's nose, cheekbones, and chin. Flattering bounce light from a 2 x 4-foot white illustration board held just above her eyes and at a distance of about 2 feet from Penny illuminated her face. Shooting handheld, I used my 105mm portrait lens, which threw the background out of focus and prevented it from being a distraction. Furthermore, the dark background provides an effective contrast to Penny's blonde hair. I exposed Tri-X film at ISO 400 for 1/250 sec. at f/5.6-8, and later had my custom lab process the film at ISO 200 to control grain.

Any agent or manager can look at Stella's headshot and remark, "She's very pretty and natural looking, and she looks like she'd be very easy to work with." An actor's ability to work comfortably with people in show business is absolutely critical in these days of spiraling production costs and very tight schedules. There is no time for prima-donna attitudes. Projecting this affability to the camera in a portrait is an integral part of the headshot process.

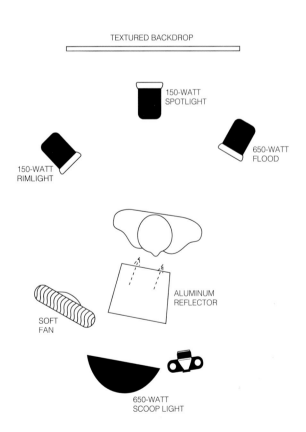

TEXTURED BACKDROP

150-WATT
SPOTLIGHT

650-WATT
FLOOD

150-WATT
RIMLIGHT

ALUMINUM
REFLECTOR

SOFT
FAN

650-WATT
SCOOP LIGHT

Stella Pierce

nny
alfour

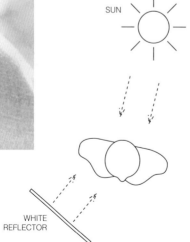

SUN

WHITE
REFLECTOR

105MM
PORTRAIT LENS
ON CAMERA

CHAPTER FIVE

PHOTOGRAPHING TWENTYSOMETHING MEN

Men's fashions vary so much in style today that it seems almost like anything goes—except, of course, for attire appropriate for the office. When it comes to selecting wardrobe for headshots, however, subjects must think in terms of moderation or, at the very least, focus. Trends, styles, and shapes come and go, of course, but certain traditional clothes are always acceptable. Any garment that is extreme attracts attention to itself and detracts from the subject's personality. Keep in mind that good taste, even in sporty clothes, is always in vogue.

I photographed Richard Welton's commercial shot outside and inside in the late afternoon. By this I mean that he was outside in a park but standing inside a tunnel. As a result, his face was illuminated by strong yet filtered sunlight coming through the open arch at the far end of the tunnel. Wearing a darker denim shirt over a gray T-shirt, Richard exudes charm through and reveals part of his personality with his infectious smile. Trained as a serious actor in New York, this headshot proves that he is qualified to do commercials, too.

Richard Welton

WARDROBE RECOMMENDATIONS

You have only to take a look at *GQ* magazine and the "Men's Fashions" section of *The New York Times* to get a clear sense of what is in style. You can also see the wide spectrum of fashions available to young leading men in advertisements for Banana Republic, Eddie Bauer, The Gap, and Tommy Hilfiger. Naturally, if expense isn't a concern, your subjects might want to consider fashions by Hugo Boss, Giorgio Armani's Le Colleszioni, and the old standby Brooks Brothers. Otherwise, subjects can opt for quality imitations of these designers' styles in order to build a great wardrobe.

I always recommend several classic styles when talking about headshots with twentysomething men. For commercial shots, I suggest a polo shirt, any open-collar oxford button-down shirt, a jean jacket over a white T-shirt, a denim shirt alone, and a scoop-neck or V-neck sweater over any kind of shirt. The wardrobe for commercial shots should be casual, outdoorsy, and sporty. Tell your clients to go with pastel shades, such as tans and medium-blue denim tones. White is all right, but off-whites are better. Be sure to have your subjects change once or twice during the commercial portion of the shoot for variety's sake.

The legit look allows for more flexibility in terms of wardrobe. A leather jacket worn over a white or black T-shirt is a popular choice, so I keep a light-brown, Italian-style leather jacket in my studio wardrobe department. This provides an alternative to the tough, black-leather-jacket image that isn't right for everyone. Another option is a Harris tweed sports jacket over an open-collared shirt. Even a simple windbreaker over a polo shirt can be attractive. Warn your clients to avoid any shirts, sweaters, or jackets that are busy with bold designs, and that it is best to stick with solid colors and very subtle or tiny plaids or stripes. When planning the legit shot with twentysomething male clients, I recommend that they wear a pair of jeans or twill pants during most of the shoot so that they stay comfortable and relaxed.

The requirements for the industrial look are minimal and somewhat rigid. This type of headshot calls for a suit, shirt, and tie, or a blazer worn over a shirt and tie. In other words, the young-executive look conjures up images of Madison Avenue and Wall Street. I usually suggest to clients that they bring a dark suit, with or without pin stripes, as well as a gray suit or jacket. Dark-blue jackets look heavy in black-and-white prints, so I tell my clients not to wear them if at all possible. If this color is a subject's only choice, I explain that he must break up the color with a white or light-blue shirt and a tie that isn't too dark either. In fact, ties should be relatively quiet and understated, with slanted stripes or tiny polka dots on silk; simply make sure that the pattern isn't outrageous or distracting.

Finally, the "leading-man" headshot is the equivalent of the glamour shot. Like its counterpart for female subjects, this photograph leaves a great deal to the imagination, too, so you can try different approaches. Leather jackets, bomber jackets, suede vests, European fashions, designer clothes, and wool outerwear are all acceptable options. As a headshot photographer, it is your responsibility to help your subjects decide what suits their image, personality, and wallet.

Eric Mattmuller's composite demonstrates all of these headshots. In his industrial shot, this handsome young man looks like a young entrepreneur (top left). He wore the requisite dark jacket and tie with tan slacks, and his serious demeanor capped off all the other elements. For his dramatic leading-man picture, Eric wanted to go with the wet look for his hair, and a dark shirt with an open collar (bottom left). He and I agreed that a turtleneck sweater and a sincere smile would work well for his commercial headshot (bottom right), while a T-shirt and a denim jacket with the collar raised a bit would give him a striking legit shot (top right). This composite is a winner.

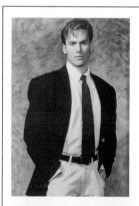

Eric Mattmuller

MAKEUP APPLICATION AND HAIRSTYLING

The makeup process is less complicated with men than it is with women. I suggest that male clients shave as close as possible for the shoot. Beards usually appear even darker than they actually are in black-and-white shots, so a close shave and a thorough application of base will minimize their appearance. I apply a pressed-powder base in a medium tone for most complexions; naturally, I use a darker base for darker skin tones. This covers most of the men's minor skin flaws. Over the base, I apply a deep terra-cotta blush to give my subjects a tanned, healthy look. This seems to work for most male faces, from the very dark to the very light skin tones.

If a male subject is skittish about wearing makeup, I explain that in any professional photographic situation, makeup always must be used. This is because bare skin reflects too much light as well as that the average face has too many flaws in it to photograph it as is. In particular, when executives begin to balk about makeup, I remind them that every politician in Washington must wear it for the television cameras. I also tell the professionals that makeup helps everyone appear more photogenic.

In terms of hairstyles for twentysomething men, I tend to work around the cut and shape my clients feel most comfortable with. James Douglas's four-picture composite shows the variety of hairstyles that you can shoot during a single session with a client. For his commercial shot, James wore a denim jacket, a white T-shirt, and his hair brushed back just a bit (top right). His hair was brushed back even more in his closeup leading-man shot, for which he turned his head (bottom left), as well as in his industrial headshot, for which he donned a suit, tie, and eyeglasses (bottom right). James went for a different look in his legit shot, switching to a black T-shirt and letting his hair hang down over the side of his head while making sure that it didn't block his eyes (top left).

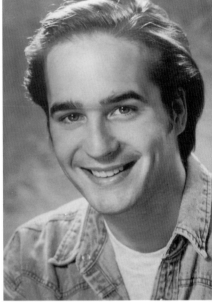

James Douglas

KEEP IT CASUAL

You'll find that some of the most appealing headshots of twentysomething men are those in which the subjects look quite casual. For these commercial shots, I instruct the men to wear, for example, a denim shirt with a tie; this creates a breezy, laid-back look that draws viewers in. The trick is to avoid any wardrobe that says "uptight." You simply have to be very careful to select wardrobe changes that suit your particular subject. When shooting casual portraits of young men, I also tell them to give me bright, sincere smiles and effervescent charm.

Tim Quill, who has appeared in several movies, was a perfect candidate for a casual commercial headshot. He comes across as a healthy All-American male or an older version of "the boy next door." Tim's good looks have a down-to-earth quality, in part because of his freckles and honest eyes. For this informal shot, he wore a gray sweatshirt and then turned on his dynamite smile.

The headshot of Steve Casserly, another up-and-coming young leading man, proves without a shadow of a doubt that he was born to do commercials. The light-toned denim jacket and white polo shirt he wore complemented his blond hair and handsome face perfectly. The final touch in this commercial shot is Steve's winning smile. In order to record his blue eyes as accurately as possible in his black-and-white headshot, I used very intense illumination. Without this, blue eyes often can look brown in a black-and-white photograph. The solution is to move the reflector or fill light in rather close in for full light saturation; then hope that your subject doesn't squint.

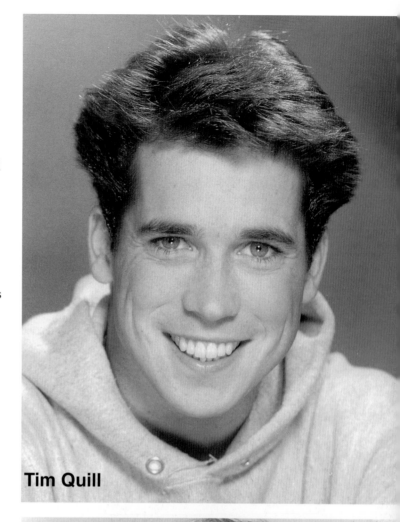

Tim Quill

Steve
Casserly

SHOOTING ON LOCATION VERSUS IN THE STUDIO

Most of the legit headshots used to secure theater, film, and television roles are shot in the photographer's studio. The association is understandable. When you think about working in any of these media, you envision enclosed spaces. For example, the legit headshot I made of standup comic/actor Terry Mulligan against a simple background in my studio works because it captures his personality and shows off his good looks and charm. I wanted this shot to look spontaneous; the rare hand-on-the-chin gesture suggests this. Here, thanks to the devilish grin on Terry's face, he seems to be holding back a laugh. I kept the lighting on the high-key side for this shot, which is the traditional comic mode.

I photographed aspiring actor L. J. Ganser's legit headshot in my studio, too. For this striking portrait, he wore a tweed blazer and a dark-blue turtleneck sweater, a wardrobe combination I usually advise against because it can appear too studied. On L. J., however, it works; this urbane outfit makes him look like a movie-channel spokesperson. To reinforce this

idea, I used rimlighting and had L. J. tilt his head and bring his fingers up to his face.

Although studio shots are more prevalent than on-location shots, this doesn't mean that you can't shoot excellent pictures outdoors. Because Craig Augustine intended to use his legit shot for soap-opera purposes, he and I thought that shooting it outside might help it stand out from the competition. I had him sit on a low-level extension next to a wall of pink and tan stone. The illumination from the sun, which was behind Craig, highlighted his hair; it also bounced off the wall to the right of his head, thereby adding a nice fill light to the shadows on the left side of his face. As I photographed him, he held a white reflector just to the right of his face. This light/shade effect works well for men because it brings out their angular bone structure. I am particularly pleased with the highlights in Craig's eyes and the great connection he made with the portrait lens. His smile, which is quieter and less toothy than it would be if this were a commercial headshot, is sincere and appealing.

Terry Mulligan

L. J. Ganser

Craig Augustine

BREAKING THE RULES

Experimenting with new techniques is essential to keep your work fresh. For example, if you automatically do the traditional head-and-shoulders portrait, try shooting a fuller view of your subject. Today, many agents and casting directors express interest in seeing three-quarter-length views of aspiring actors, so I shoot a large-format shot during each session. Keep in mind, however, that you may have to give young, insecure actors more direction than usual. Be prepared to answer the question, "What do I do with my hands?"

I photographed a full view of Phoenix Adonis in my studio. This strong portrait shows that even the most basic of costumes can be effective. To bring out the dimensions of Phoenix's handsome, angular face and to emphasize his cheekbones, I placed two 150-watt rimlights about 3 feet behind his shoulders and 2 feet above his head. This resulted in highlights on either side of his face. Then I directed Phoenix to fold his arms across his chest in order to feature his muscular build. This shot is simple but powerful.

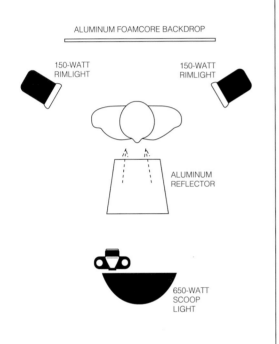

Phoenix Adonis

THE YOUNG EXECUTIVE LOOK

Today, high-powered executives are no longer easily identified by age, gender, or race. It isn't out of the realm of possibility for a corporate type to be young, female, and/or African, Asian, or Hispanic, among other races. But one stereotype associated with the corporate world remains. This is the corporate look, which requires a business suit.

For this three-quarter-length industrial shot, Ben Brian wore a Hugo Boss suit and tie. He looks like the young vice president of a dynamic new company whose stock just went public. His big smile and confident pose suggest that he is happy about the good news. I made this shot across the street from my studio in a doorway to a beautiful building that can suggest a college or business atmosphere. Ben stood in the shade, and an aluminum reflector bounced additional light onto his figure. I shot this large-format portrait with a 50mm lens from a slightly lower angle than usual to make Ben appear a little taller. This successful industrial headshot could cross over into the commercial category.

Ben Brian

THE TOUGH LOOK

Once in a while, an actor wants a headshot that reflects his tough side in addition to the four traditional portraits. Some aspiring performers intend to submit this picture for specific jobs, such as roles on television police dramas or films with storylines involving criminals. A part playing the sinister other man in a soap-opera love triangle is another possibility. When you work with clients, remember that the tough-guy shot shouldn't be too heavy; it should have something of a romantic quality to it.

Kevin Cornell's legit headshot, which I made in my studio, reflects a tough persona. He looks dramatic and a bit ominous here; nevertheless, his dark good looks reinforce his appeal as a young leading man. I decided to create a Los Angeles tan, but I didn't need too much base because of his flawless complexion. To achieve the tough-guy effect, Kevin applied a little mousse to his hair. The stray strands of hair dangling over his forehead enhance his sexy/dangerous image. The black leather jacket, complete with zippers, adds the finishing touch.

Kevin Cornell

HOLLYWOOD SEX APPEAL

Exuding sex appeal and irresistible charm is what this type of headshot is all about. To get twentysomething men to do this successfully, I tell them to concentrate solely on the lover playing opposite them in a love scene. This is the kind of intense gaze that this Hollywood look demands. Be prepared to come across actors who are unable to do this. In these situations, you might want to tell them to emulate box-office stars who have perfected this skill, such as Alec Baldwin.

One client who has mastered the fine art of projecting a sexy image is handsome Michael C. Pierce. A veteran of many print advertisements and commercials, he is a consummate professional; his range of experience is evident. Lighting someone who has exceptional bone structure is always easy, and my basic key-light/fill-light/backlight combination worked to great advantage with Michael. For this legit headshot, he pulled his look together by wearing a tan cashmere sweater over a striped shirt. Here, however, the "eyes have it."

Maurizio De Maurizi is another aspiring actor with plenty of charm. For this leading-man shot, he wore a black windbreaker over a denim shirt, as well as a very loose tie. His easygoing nature adds to his appeal. Although I don't ordinarily use a fan on male clients, I wanted a bit of outdoor movement to enhance Maurizio's special electricity.

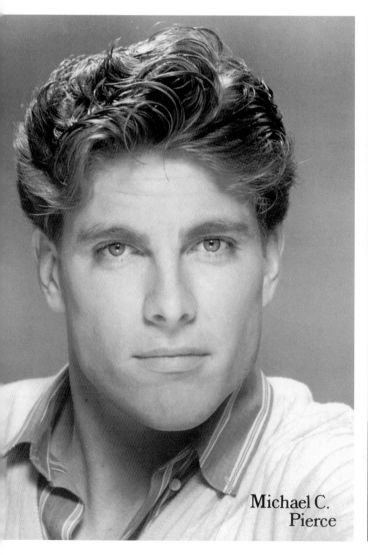

Michael C.
Pierce

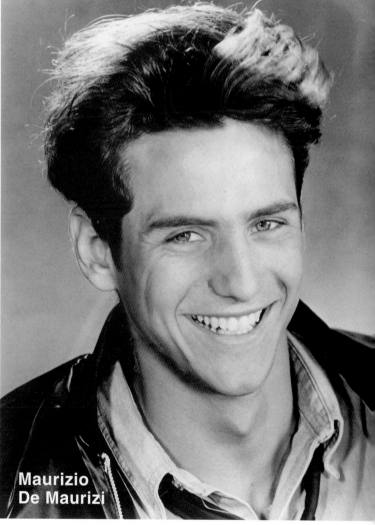

Maurizio
De Maurizi

CATCH A RISING STAR

Some actors start their careers as standup comics. Think of Tom Hanks, Steve Martin, and Eddie Murphy, to name a few. These men belong to a special group of actors who know comic timing and how to build to a punch line, and yet still are able to deliver a credible performance in a dramatic role. During a shooting session with a performer who specializes in standup comedy, you have to search for those magic moments when they become their quintessential selves. Having performers do their actual material for you is one of the best ways to get them to relax and to manifest their rare talent. This requires a delicate balance between too much energy and too little.

With Jim Breuer, I found out that just the right turn of the head to the camera can become an over-the-shoulder shot with a comic twist. The look in his eye reveals a certain kind of humor ready to explode at any second. Jim wore a dark sports shirt under a dark-brown leather jacket. Since he wasn't wearing a motorcycle-type jacket, the picture doesn't look too much like a put-on. His somewhat tousled hair adds another quirk to the comic image, which I wanted to be freewheeling and adventurous. I selected a graded neutral-gray background for this shot. I illuminated Jim frontally and added the backlight to pull him away from the backdrop and to highlight his hair.

Jim Breuer

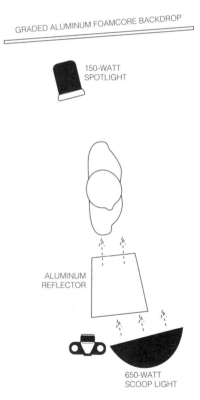

GRADED ALUMINUM FOAMCORE BACKDROP

150-WATT SPOTLIGHT

ALUMINUM REFLECTOR

650-WATT SCOOP LIGHT

GETTING TO THE TOP OF THE CHARTS

Lou
Taylor
Rox

While working with aspiring musician Lou Taylor Rox, I decided to capture a variety of movements and expressions. I felt that a picture depicting action would capture his energy, good looks, and talent at their dynamic best (left). Lou certainly knows how to play to the camera, so recording that kind of spark was easy. This profile shot would be perfect for a compact-disc cover; it would also work well on a composite, suggesting how the performer looks on stage.

Since Lou looks good no matter what he wears, wardrobe was never a primary concern during this session. I simply made sure that I photographed him in the customary number of outfits. For his legit shot, Lou wore a sports shirt with a graphic design, which was bold but not too busy (below). Because of his intense gaze and serious expression, he looks quite different from the singer in the action shot. Both shots, however, show off Lou to great advantage.

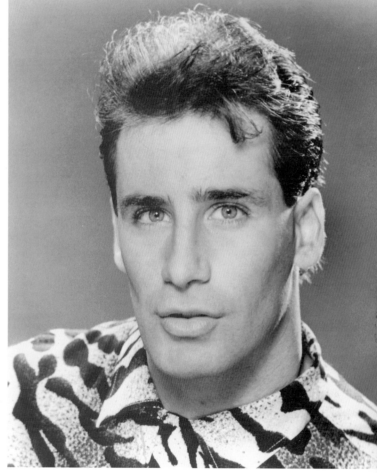

IN CHARACTER

Making a set of headshots for actor J. J. Reap proved to be an unusual experience. When he told me that did readings from Charles Dickens's work in a one-man-show format, I thought that it would be fun to take on a real challenge. So in addition to shooting the traditional headshots, I decided to photograph J. J. made up as Dickens. The resulting contrast in appearance is striking—and was fun to achieve. For J. J.'s industrial headshot, he wore a dark suit and tie (left). I had him hold a pair of eyeglasses because I thought this prop would add authenticity. Here, I chose a fuller-length format and a deep neutral-gray background.

Next, I started transforming J. J. into one of the greatest Victorian novelists. While I did the makeup application, I kept in mind that my subject would be seen on stage, where distance helps to blend details. As such, I didn't make him up as I would have for a film closeup. Here, the period costume; the graying hair; the age lines in the forehead, around the mouth, and under the eyes; and the spirit-gummed beard successfully bring Dickens back to life for theatrical performances. Try to create a character in full makeup once and awhile. If nothing else, it will make your day-to-day makeup chores seem like a breeze.

J. J. Reap

J. J. Reap as Charles Dickens

THINK OF THE POSSIBILITIES

When you photograph clients, it is important to consider the various types of looks you can help them achieve. For example, Alan Tulin is a versatile performer who can play a number of parts, including that of a young character actor, comic, business executive, and leading man. In one shot, which I made in my studio, Alan's comic possibilities assert themselves (right). Using only a pen as a prop, he readily personifies the looks that reveals a professional with a sense of humor. His wide-eyed expression and pursed lips reinforce his lighthearted approach to this headshot.

To provide Alan with an effective legit shot, I planned to work outside in available light (below). Here, he looks like a little older and a little wiser than he does in his comic shot. Alan switched eyeglasses for this serious picture, and they serve to make him come across as honest and above board; viewers would trust him with their municipal bonds. Whether Alan wears a dark suit and tie or a sporty jacket with an open-collared shirt, he always makes his outfit an integral part of the persona he is creating.

ALAN
TULIN
541-7600

Alan Tulin

LIGHTING TECHNIQUES

I prefer natural lighting or studio lighting that mimics that type of illumination for my headshot photography. When devising an athletic look for Brian Thurston, I planned to shoot his pictures outdoors. For this three-quarter-length shot, he wore a polo shirt and a pair of shorts, and looks like he is about to play tennis. He has a marvelous way with the camera, his eye contact is exceptional, and his quiet strength qualifies him for the young-leading-man label. As I directed Brian to lean against a wall in Riverside Park, I made sure to keep the background neutral so that it wouldn't be a distraction. The bright sky provided very strong fill/bounce light coming in at Brian from the open end of the tunnel. As such, I didn't have to use a reflector gave me more flexibility as I shot.

Although I am partial to the effect of available light, whether it occurs naturally or is duplicated indoors, I know that it is possible to creatively illuminate subjects in the studio. For this commercial headshot, Lou Toscano switched out of his rock-star wardrobe (see page 89) into a smart tuxedo. He appears to be dressed for a concert. Lou's big smile helps to establish this picture as a leading-man shot. This happy performer is turning on the charm for his fans. I wanted to establish a theatrical or cabaret mood for this closeup portrait, so I positioned a 650-watt spotlight slightly to Lou's right in order to shade his handsome face. Tight cropping increased the graphic impact of this image, which is essential when headshot pictures are used for publicity purposes.

Brian
Thurston

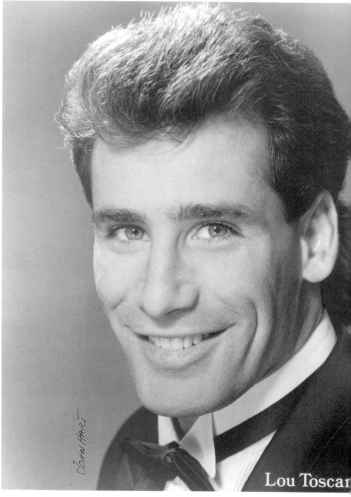

Lou Toscar

Joseph Corbin's legit headshot is an exciting combination of natural light and artificial-light sources. In September the direct rays of the sun pour into my New York City studio at just the right angle during the late afternoon as the sun starts to descend. To take complete advantage of this light, I had Joseph lean against the studio wall adjacent to the source of sunlight on his right. This position illuminated his head and torso with intense sidelighting. I balanced this strong simulated sunlight by pointing my 650-watt scoop light almost directly at him. This eliminated dark, distracting shadows that might obscure facial and clothing details. Joseph wore a tank top for this informal three-quarter-length shot, although some agents, managers, and photographers might not approve. Individual preferences and the specific part an actor is up for will greatly influence the decision-making process. Remember, good taste should always dominate.

STUDIO WALL

STUDIO WINDOW

650-WATT SCOOP LIGHT

Joseph Corbin

CHAPTER SIX

PHOTOGRAPHING THIRTYSOMETHING WOMEN

No matter how old performers are, they should choose a look that suits their age. This outward appearance should be appropriate in terms of wardrobe, hairstyling, and makeup. For example, actresses shouldn't dress to take 10 years off their age; this mistake can often make them look either foolish or even older than they actually are. To avoid this problem, leading ladies need only to check out the fashion statements being made by designers who cater to their age range. This will enable actresses in their twenties to move gracefully into the next decade, as well as permit those already in their thirties to get an idea of what is in style and what is in good taste.

In her glamour shot, Cleo Coppa proves just how effective a headshot that accurately reflects your age can be. When selecting her wardrobe,

she decided on an attractive, V-neck gold-lamé gown. This dress framed her chiseled features beautifully. I used a deep-rose blush under Cleo's prominent cheekbones to highlight them. Then I determined that a simple, straight-on, relaxed gaze would work best for her. Finally, I had a medium-speed fan blow her hair off her face to emphasize her cheekbones even more.

The result: a stunning look for a 30-year-old.

Cleo Coppa

WARDROBE RECOMMENDATIONS

When discussing appropriate attire for headshots with thirtysomething women, I suggest clothing traditionally associated with each type of picture. For commercial shots, casual, open-collared pastel shirts or blouses are fine. For legit shots, less sporty or outdoorsy tops, such as sweaters and scoop-neck blouses, are good; colors here can be a little darker than they are in commercial shots. And, of course, industrial shots require a business look: suits, white blouses, and simple jewelry.

Your thirtysomething subjects have a great deal of leeway—and can have a lot of fun—when selecting wardrobe for their glamour shots. Tell your clients to think cabaret: formal gowns, bare shoulders, diamond drop earrings, and chunky gold necklaces. In other words, they can try to achieve an elegant, somewhat extravagant look.

Rosemary Pascale's industrial shot is perfect (left). She looks quite attractive, thanks in part to her great eyes and sensitive eye contact. She wore a dark jacket with a white silk blouse and folded her arms. The silk handkerchief in the jacket pocket sets off the entire image. I helped finish her makeup. Keep in mind that a little extra gloss on the center of the lower lip brings more life and dimension to a subject's mouth. Apply gloss rather liberally for glamour shots; use less for industrial pictures.

For Rosemary's other headshot, she assumed a much more relaxed pose (right). For this commercial picture, she chose a simple scoop-neck blouse and small gold earrings. Rosemary's bright smile combines with her brushed-forward bangs to create a youthful, vibrant image.

ROSEMARY
PASCALE

MAKEUP APPLICATION AND HAIRSTYLING

A mood swing accompanied by minimal hairstyle, makeup, and costume changes can provide you with all the contrast that you need during a shoot. You simply have to encourage or instruct your subject to display a variety of emotions and create the perfect setting for this to take place. Varying your client's physical appearance is critical, too. In essence, then, you must fulfill the role of photographer as well as that of director, producer, set designer, analyst, and best boy. Try not to be overwhelmed by this prospect; challenges are always fun, aren't they? Keeping an open mind helps those creative juices flow even more freely.

When I planned Charlotte Osawa's session with her, we agreed that her headshots should reflect her vitality and energy. For her terrific glamour shot, she wore a dark suit (no blouse) and pearl earrings (right). Her hair was swept up and away from her forehead. Her large blue eyes attract viewers to her immediately. She comes across as sexy without having to try too hard. In contrast, I decided to try something really different for her commercial shot (left). When she laughed out loud during our conversation, I told her to turn her head slightly away from the key light. The result was a headshot that seems to redefine the word spontaneous.

CHARLOTTE
OSAWA

CHARLOTTE
OSAWA

CAPTURING A CLIENT'S PERSONALITY

Gabrielle Widman

Christine Taylor

When you work with performers, you should take full advantage of their unique looks and styles. By tapping into your subjects, you'll be stimulated to go beyond the mundane portrait work that is so prevalent. In turn, you'll be able to reflect your clients' true personalities and provide them with four different but accurate depictions of themselves.

One of the best smiles I've ever seen belongs to Gabrielle Widman. For this commercial shot, she wore a dark V-neck top. As I photographed her, I told her to look slightly over her left shoulder at the camera; I also instructed her to repeat one of my favorite lines, "This orange juice tastes delicious!" I pressed the shutter as soon as I heard the "s" in delicious. What you see here is a portrait that captures Gabrielle's personality at its effervescent best.

Christine Taylor's legit headshot is a quintessential example of the fan shot. This glamorous portrait has everything a casting director could ask for: a beautiful woman with blonde hair, blue eyes, and a dynamic sense of style. Christine's choice of a beige, scoop-neck silk blouse sets off her elegant, long neck.

THREE LEADING LADIES

Commercial portraits of thirtysomething women are crucial to their ability to obtaining potentially lucrative work as leading ladies. Paula Heitman has been modeling and acting since she was six years old. Her skill at interacting with the camera is clear proof of this experience. Her freshness and outgoing personality make her an ideal candidate for a leading-lady role. Paula always has a special sparkle in her eyes that allows her to come across as particularly exuberant in her photographs. Film and soap-opera actress Karen Lynn Gorney is another performer who exudes professionalism. The combination of her charismatic eye contact with the camera and her fabulous face makes for a knockout commercial headshot.

Paula Heitman

Karen Lynn Gorney

Jennifer Dente is a talented singer/actress, as well as an ideal leading lady. Her luminous eyes and bright smile light up any room—and stage. For this combination glamour/commercial headshot, Jennifer wore a velvet top with an unusual neckline; the result is a romantic effect. This look is in keeping with her sweet face. The lighting design I chose for Jennifer highlights her curly mass of dark hair. I aimed a 150-watt spotlight with a diffuser at the back of her head to create a soft glow around her hair. While shooting, I directed Jennifer to tilt her head slightly to the right to show off her shiny tresses even more. Next, I aimed another 150-watt light at the foamcore backdrop, but I didn't put a diffuser on this lamp. A 650-watt scoop light and an aluminum reflector under my subject's chin provided the frontlighting and fill light, respectively.

Jennifer Dente

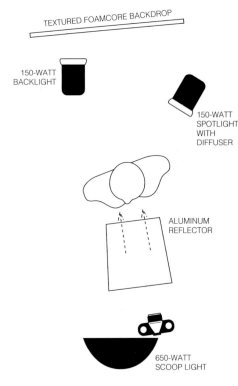

TEXTURED FOAMCORE BACKDROP

150-WATT BACKLIGHT

150-WATT SPOTLIGHT WITH DIFFUSER

ALUMINUM REFLECTOR

650-WATT SCOOP LIGHT

THE FEMALE EXECUTIVE

Wearing a dark tweed suit with a white shirt, Marla Bingham certainly comes across as a professional in charge of the situation. Her quiet self-confidence is evident in this industrial shot. Here, she stands (rather than sits) with her arms folded, looking like a business executive about to make an announcement to the board of directors, or a prosecuting attorney about to present her closing argument to the jury. Marla projects this corporate image quite well. Getting her to do this was only a matter of her concentrating on a specific role and my giving her a small amount of direction as I shot.

When I photographed Robin Simmen, she and I agreed to try a variation of the industrial portrait; the resulting picture integrates elements of the commercial and glamour headshots. She wore a teal silk blouse and gold earrings, and her hair was brushed up and off her face. Robin's warm smile pulls the shot together; she looks like an executive with heart.

MARLA BINGHAM

Robin Simmen

A TOUCH OF GLAMOUR

Glamour, like beauty, is in the eyes of the beholder. Although what constitutes glamour is a matter of personal preference, most people can agree that a basic standard exists. Allure, which is a synonym for glamour, always conjures up images of attractive, bewitching people who know how to effectively combine a persona, hairstyle, makeup, and wardrobe to appear appealing. They create a special, distinctive look for themselves.

Bao-Guo Wang is an opera singer whose beauty adds to her appealing presence. For this glamour shot, she and I agreed that capturing her great smile was critical to the impact her picture would have.

Furthermore, because I know that her soprano voice has graced many opera stages, I wanted to suggest that upper-echelon world of red carpets, crystal chandeliers, and Puccini al fresco. The sweetheart neckline that Bao wore added to this sense of opulence. The finishing touch was the effect of her fan-blown long tresses.

When planning this shot, I felt that a textured background hit with a 150-watt light at shoulder height would work. For backlighting, I positioned a 600-watt flood behind Bao's left shoulder. To illuminate her from the front, I aimed a 650-watt lamp at her face and tilted a reflector under her chin. A flag was placed slightly in front of Bao on her left side.

Bao-Guo Wang

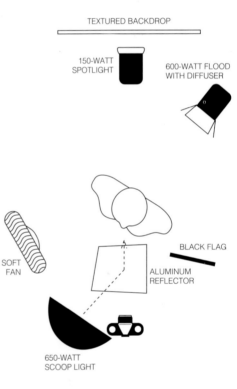

TEXTURED BACKDROP

150-WATT
SPOTLIGHT

600-WATT FLOOD
WITH DIFFUSER

SOFT
FAN

BLACK FLAG

ALUMINUM
REFLECTOR

650-WATT
SCOOP LIGHT

THE PERFORMANCE PICTURE

Photographs of a performer seemingly at work can gives agents and clients a true sense of what that individual is capable of. As such, you should pay close attention to detail when doing these shots for your clients. For example, when I photographed Karey Hall, I made sure that her makeup was flattering and that her wardrobe was ideally suited to her. Together, we chose a beaded V-neck gown and crystal drop earrings. They provided the touch of glamour she needed to make this a suitable headshot for her career in the opera. To open up Karey's face a bit and make this portrait more dramatic, I used my fan. Her intense expression puts the finishing touch on this opera-diva image.

When working with rock singer D. J. Daly, I knew that I had to capture this new talent's dazzle in her headshot. For her combination glamour/legit picture, I then instructed her to look over her right shoulder directly at the camera. I told her to lean slightly forward into the main light and to look seductive and alluring. Next, my subject and I agreed that a simple hairstyle would work well, so we brushed back her long blonde hair. I then backlit it with a 650-watt spotlight positioned on D. J.'s left and allowed the fan to style it. Finally, I darkened D. J.'s lipstick and added more eyeshadow, mascara, and eyeliner. Round gold earrings complete this "moving" picture.

Karey Hall

D. J. Daly

LIGHTING TECHNIQUES

Effectively illuminating thirtysomething leading ladies requires the standard lighting configuration, including a main light, back light, and fill light. On my main light, I use two diffusion screens to prevent the light from being too harsh on anyone. On the rare occasions when I want to soften the illumination even more as a subject's age or complexion requires, I add a medium hair filter to my 105mm portrait lens. Agents want realism in headshots, not idealistic fantasies.

In terms of lighting, the only difference you'll notice when you work with thirtyish women is that some of the subjects in this group have more hair and call for more intense illumination. You need to make sure that the overall effect is light and airy—almost high key—not dark and dismal. This holds true no matter what type of complexion your clients have. Of course, they should look like themselves; however, your job is to make them look their best, nothing less. When actors land a part, a great deal of attention is paid to their makeup and hair in order to present them to the public in the most flattering way possible. Remember this when doing headshots for them.

Leigh Anne O'Connor exemplifies that fresh, "walking through the park on a brisk day" feeling that

I think translates so well in headshots, particularly commercial and legit pictures. For this commercial shot, my subject sported an open-collared denim shirt; she didn't wear any jewelry, not even earrings, because I didn't want anything to detract from her. This picture succeeds because of Leigh Anne's fresh, open outlook; her wonderful eye contact; and her carefully applied makeup, which emphasizes her eyes, lips, and skin texture without being excessive.

Here, I chose one of my favorite backgrounds, a piece of brushed-aluminum foamcore, which I rubbed with a steel-wool pad to tone down its shiny surface. Because this 8 x 10-foot board is so lightweight, I can turn it in different directions to get less or more reflection as needed. For this shot of Leigh Anne, I wanted a subtle overcast-sky effect, not a distracting glow in the background. In addition, I rotated the background so the dark section that is usually at the top behind my client's head is on the right side, and the lighter part, which is ordinarily behind the person's shoulders, is to the left. This original twist broke the monotony of my routine. Finally, as usual, the hair light helped to separate the subject's head from the background and gave her long tresses lovely highlights.

BRUSHED-ALUMINUM FOAMCORE BACKDROP

150-WATT
SPOTLIGHT

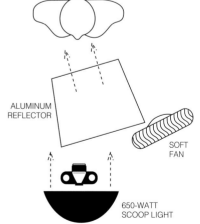
ALUMINUM
REFLECTOR

SOFT
FAN

650-WATT
SCOOP LIGHT

Leigh Anne
O'Connor

Victoria
Kelly

Victoria Kelly's headshots prove that less can indeed be more. As you can see, she wore minimal makeup and a simple outfit. She also had a devil-may-care, gamine hairstyle that suited her perfectly. With her exceptional good looks and sparkling smile, she was more than a pleasure to work with.

Victoria's commercial shot is all sweetness and light (left), which, when compared to her rather serious legit shot (bottom), reveals two personas. I knew that I wanted to achieve an almost high-key, bounce lighting, the kind of illumination you see inside on a bright summer day. This was an unusual lighting plan for these two types of headshots; the goal is ordinarily more subdued.

Another reverse involves Victoria's wardrobe. She wore a V-neck top for her commercial shot instead of her legit shot, as you would expect. Similarly, the denim shirt that you would expect to see in the casual commercial shot appears in her legit shot. Although this variation in customary attire had no apparent effect on the lighting, it contributed to the moods of the two shots. This ambiguous, unexpected break from the norm increased the power of the pictures.

Light your subjects' hair, especially if it is blonde. Then go ahead and light their skin and their clothes. All of these elements demand light, particularly when shot in black and white. Wouldn't you rather see a brilliantly illuminated photograph than a dark, murky one? I know that agents and casting people would. They don't want to guess about what shade of hair or skin actors have, nor do they want to wonder about makeup tones or the colors of a performer's clothes. They want a realistic image, not a brooding, fashion-photography interpretation.

Victoria Kelly

CHAPTER SEVEN

PHOTOGRAPHING THIRTYSOMETHING MEN

When men reach their thirties, their faces evolve and become more mature-looking, and their bone structure often becomes more defined. In addition, the men themselves develop an outlook on life and on the business of acting that is both wiser and more worldly than the one they had in their twenties. These major changes are advantageous for headshot photographers. And in fact, many casting people say that an actor only really starts to work when he turns 30.

This idea is valid. Consider, for example, that many theater-trained performers have to apprentice for 10 to 15 years before they're even taken seriously as actors. Furthermore, many film actors get their best roles during their thirties; think of Al Pacino, Robert de Niro, Dustin Hoffman, and Paul Newman, just to name a few. As such, growing older gives male performers more and better opportunities to work at their chosen craft.

Rick Siegel, a popular pianist who plays at all of the top spots in New York City, has an air of sophistication. This demeanor, combined with his handsome face, demanded a leading-man shot. For this portrait, Rick pulled out all the stops and wore a tuxedo. Perhaps what makes this headshot so compelling is his ability to seem personable and warm at the same time that he comes across as urbane.

Rick
Siegel

WARDROBE RECOMMENDATIONS

As a headshot photographer, you'll find yourself continually facing creative challenges. Although the portraits you shoot have their own strictures and demands, sometimes you may want to try a different and possibly surprising technique. Simply make sure that your approach keeps its pulse on your subject's personality. Have fun with this, particularly when you help clients choose their wardrobe. Although you should follow the traditional guidelines for the four types of headshots, you may want to veer off course a bit for one picture. Recommend, for example, that your subject substitute a high-quality undershirt for an open-collared denim shirt in his commercial shot, or a tuxedo for suit jacket in his leading-man shot. To prevent an industrial shot from looking too rigid, have your client wear, perhaps, a button-down oxford shirt, a silk scarf, and a dark-blue silk jacket. As long as you don't carry these variations to an extreme, you'll discover that experimentation is always good.

During a shoot, I often suggest something out of the ordinary. I may try a different lighting design, or I may direct my subject to turn an unusual way. Otherwise, I may have a client put on a silly hat just to break the two of us up and lighten the mood on the set. Of

John
Unruh

course, I tell my subjects that if we don't like the end result, we don't have to use it. I maintain that a little diversion might give an extra spark to the basic work at hand; renew the clients' energy level and interest in the session; and/or stimulate a new, more intimate contact with the camera on their part.

For actor John Unruh's legit headshot, he wore a light-blue polo shirt that was perfect for this outdoor portrait. I made this picture in open shade in front of my building. Here, John, who was looking directly into the sun, held a reflector at chest level to lighten the shading on his face. I decided to capitalize on his handsome face and penetrating gaze. His very serious demeanor is more intense than that typically seen in this kind of headshot. John's two strong features are prerequisites for beating out the competition in the acting profession.

THE PICTURE OF HEALTH

Many actors are always on the go. They realize that in order to give a sparkling, high-energy performance, they have to stay in top physical condition. To that end, they work out regularly, eat right, and try to maintain a positive attitude—despite the vagaries of the entertainment field.

In Bill Lee's legit headshot, he looks as if he were on his yacht gazing at the shoreline near Monaco. Because he is an outdoor type who is in great physical shape, the two of us agreed that this should be visible in his

headshot. I broke one rule while working with this subject: I photographed Bill looking directly at the sun. When I saw him turn this way, I made this shot very quickly. For balance, however, I took two shots of him posing in shaded light and looking directly into the camera. Bill combined these for an effective composite. As this portrait shows, the parameters for legit headshots aren't as restrictive as you might think. They are, in fact, conducive to a wide range of imaginative interpretations.

Bill Lee

108

THE FACIAL-HAIR QUESTION

Certain men think that they might look better sporting a mustache, goatee, or beard. When photographing with these subjects, I suggest that I take some shots of them with facial hair and some without, and then study the contact sheets to determine which way they look best. Of course, some men think that they look older or more masculine with a mustache, while a few others use one to camouflage a split lip. Similarly, some men grow beards to hide a weak chin or jaw line. Although you must ultimately adhere to the "to each his own" dictum as far as facial hair is concerned, you should tell male clients that mustaches are rarely seen in commercials. You should also ask your subjects if they really want to stand out because they look atypical. Point out that it might be better to let a director decide if a specific part calls for facial hair or a scruffy look.

One solution to the facial-hair question is to put together a composite that shows at least three different looks for a client. When working outside with Frank Pisciotta, I took a rugged shot of him with a mustache (bottom left). I then had him go inside to shave it off and photographed him again (right). Finally, I took a straight-on industrial headshot (top left). The resulting composite shows how Frank looks with a mustache, but the two clean-shaven shots prevent this from dominating his image.

As his portrait shows, stand-up comic Eddie Clark is another thirtysomething man who wears a mustache. Fortunately, he looks great with it; it seems to serve as a frame for his big smile in this commercial headshot. Capturing a sense of humor on film can be quite a challenge, so I let Eddie perform a bit of his routine. Typically, this relaxed him and enabled me to record his special spark and comedic flair.

A final point about facial hair. Every once in a while, a subject wants me to photograph him unshaven. In these situations, I tell my client not to shave on the morning of the session, during which I take only 12 to 20 such shots. The subject then shaves off his light beard, and I resume shooting immediately, usually with him wearing the same shirt.

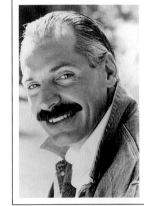

Frank Pisciotta

Eddie Clark

IN THE SPOTLIGHT

Performers yearn for center stage, no matter what form it takes. And to give agents and casting people a clear idea of their versatility, actors need headshots that showcase their talents and capture the different aspects of their personality. Keep in mind, too, that show business has numerous offshoots and areas of interest, many of which demand special talents. Simply think of the unions that cover these fields, such as Actors' Equity, the Screen Actors Guild, the American Federation of Television and Radio Artists, and the American Federation of Musicians. As a headshot photographer, you must be ready to give all performers headshots that will effectively represent them in their respective fields.

Craig Schulman's headshots make two specific and distinct impressions. He looks somewhat serious in his legit shot, which he could submit for television, film, and even some commercial jobs (left). Here, he has down-home-country appeal. Craig's leading-man picture, which is a direct contrast to this legit shot, indicates that he can appear suave and sophisticated as well (right). His gaze is quite intense. For this shot, he changed into a tuxedo to complete the look that is appropriate for Broadway and concert work.

Craig
Schulman

MR. EXECUTIVE

The industrial headshot is important for thirtysomething men. They seem well suited to the role of corporate executive.

Model Paul Linnell is handsome and has a commanding presence, as this legit shot reveals. The lighting design I utilized here was rather simple. Working without a hair light, I positioned a 650-watt light in front of Paul and slightly to his right. Then I bounced this light off a tilted reflector that was also in front of my subject but off to his left a bit. I aimed a 150-watt light at the unobtrusive textured background I'd selected.

Put him in a suit and tie, and he becomes the quintessential business executive. He looks very authoritative and distinguished, largely because of the intensity of his gaze and the deliberate turn of his head. Paul's chiseled features also help to set this industrial headshot apart.

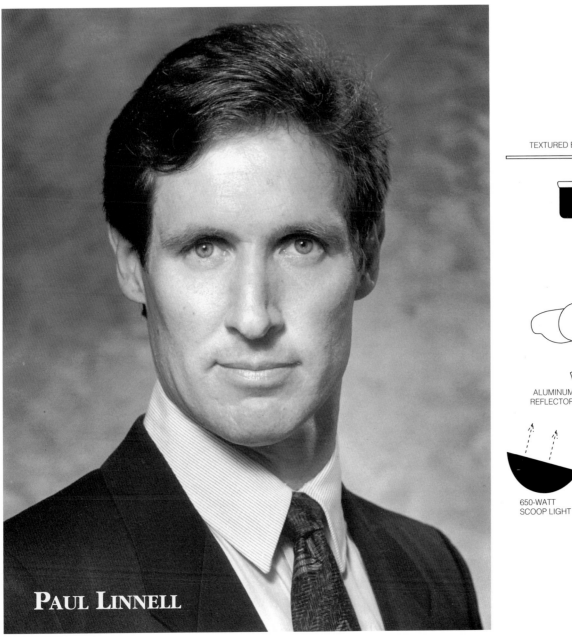

PAUL LINNELL

TEXTURED BACKDROP

150-WATT
SPOTLIGHT

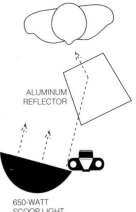

ALUMINUM
REFLECTOR

650-WATT
SCOOP LIGHT

LIGHTING TECHNIQUES

One of the most important lessons you need to learn when working with male clients is that you don't have to backlight their hair as much as that of female clients. Most men have far less hair than women, so they don't require illumination of comparable intensity. Usually, one 150-watt hair light will highlight the hair on either side of a male subject's part adequately.

Thanks to these commercial headshots, you can begin to understand who these actors are without knowing anything about their lives. You can get a clear sense of their individual natures and the way they deal with the open, outgoing, salesperson style that is the essence of the Madison Avenue commercial look. Each subject has a distinctive type of personality projection, which results in winning headshots. Michael Broughton has a captivating smile and a vital persona that could encourage people to buy just about any product—and to hire him for acting jobs. When photographing Michael, I decide to use a simple lighting design: a key light, a soft hair light, and a reflector.

Michael Broughton

Another thirtysomething male performer with a wonderful presence is pianist Buck Buckholz. He asked me to take photographs of him for the cover and inside notes of his new album. Since he'd had a tape of his favorite songs digitally recorded during a live session, he and I felt that it would be appropriate to take the shots "on the job." To keep the performance mood going, I wanted to utilize the available spotlighting in the Oak Room at New York City's famous Algonquin Hotel, where Buck was performing. As a result, I needed to bring only my trusty Nikon with me to the shoot, not any lighting equipment.

I knew that because of the low intensity of the room's illumination, I would have to shoot time exposures to let enough light reach the film. Exposing Kodak Tri-X Pan film, with a film-speed rating of ISO 400, for 1/15 sec. at *f*/4, I shot handheld. I wanted to

move around a great deal as I worked in order to see Buck from various vantage points in the audience, so I didn't use a tripod. I braced myself against the wall for this medium-length shot of Buck sitting at the keys for the inside of the insert in the cassette case. Here, I worked with just two lights, the key light and the backlight at the piano.

What keeps headshot photographers interested in and excited about their work is the continuous flow of unique individuals who come to their studio. Some are perfect leading men, while some are wonderful character types. You must be willing and able to work with them to bring out their best. Finally, keep in mind that this age range can be particularly rewarding because the men have gained a maturity that is quite appealing, and often makes them more photogenic now than when they were younger.

150-WATT SPOTLIGHT

300-WATT KEY LIGHT

Buck Buckholz

CHAPTER EIGHT

PHOTOGRAPHING OLDER WOMEN

When women reach the forty-plus age bracket, ingenue roles are, of course, inappropriate for them. But growing older doesn't mean that these leading ladies won't be able to find work. Like older male actors, they'll discover that many new and challenging roles await them. As a matter of fact, many mature actresses feel that they're working more now on soap operas and in commercials than ever before. As a headshot photographer, you'll note that female performers in this age range are quieter and more serious than their younger counterparts; they also have much more going on behind the eyes. In addition, older women have learned through trial and error how to present themselves to their best advantage in terms of their hair, makeup, and wardrobe.

Michelle Ferguson comes across as a classy woman wearing a casual outfit in her commercial headshot. Her open-collared, striped shirt and small earrings work well together. When planning the lighting design for Michelle, I decided to illuminate her basically straight on from the front with a scoop light. A reflector tilted under her chin provided fill light. Finally, I wanted to keep the backlighting minimal because there was enough light reflecting up front, so I simply aimed two 150-watt lights at Michelle's brunette hair and then let her do the rest! Her smile is warm and appealing.

Michelle Ferguson

WARDROBE RECOMMENDATIONS

In terms of wardrobe for headshots, older leading ladies should wear clothes that are suited to their age range. For the most part, trying to dress in order to compete with their younger counterparts is a mistake. The only exception to this is a denim shirt, which is appropriate for everyone. Mature women should strive for a tailored look: simple necklines, no fussy frills, no busy stripes or floral patterns. Ideally, these subjects should wear neutral shades, such as beige, tan, and light blue and pink. Older women should avoid black as much as possible. When it comes to fabric, they should think "soft"; cashmeres and silks are great choices. Finally, these performers should opt for little if any jewelry. Of course, small earrings and pearl necklaces are acceptable.

As I always recommend to my clients, Pamela Brooks brought several different styles of wardrobe with her to the shooting session. For her commercial shot, she chose a dark, scoop-neck top (below). Its texture and drop shoulders suit the casual mood of this picture. She decided to forgo earrings here. Pamela then changed into a light-colored sequined top for her legit shot (right). She left a few buttons on this dressy top open; she also added a pair of gold earrings.

When you shoot in the three-quarter-length format, as I did for Pamela's legit photograph, keep in mind that you have to adjust the lighting setup used for head-and-shoulders closeups. If you don't pull the main light up and back a bit, all the lights will show in the frame. This is because either you've switched from a 105mm lens to a 50mm lens in order to get a fuller view of your subject, or you've moved the camera back in order to see more of the torso in the frame. Be aware that you might have to open up half a stop or so in these situations for two reasons. The key light throws less light on the subject, and the reflector bounces less light on the subject because it is farther away from the face. But if your client is seated, the backlight intensities will stay the same; however, if your client stands and you shoot from the elbows up, you'll have to raise the backlights to match the higher key light.

Pamela Brooks

Pamela Brooks

MAKEUP APPLICATION AND HAIRSTYLING

To see a typical hair-and-makeup styling change for older leading ladies, take a look at the headshots of Ann McCormack, an actress/country-western singer who frequently performs in clubs and cabarets in the New York City area. She wore a black vest and plaid denim shirt for her first shot, the commercial picture (below). Her long, curly hair was loose and full in keeping with the Texas feeling she and I wanted to establish. At this stage, I used minimal makeup for a fresh look. Ann has great bone structure and wonderful dimples, so I didn't need to do much contouring at this point; I simply applied a deep-pink blush to her cheeks. The overall effect is friendly and inviting.

As you can see in Ann's glamour headshot, I increased her makeup (right). Here, I added some eye shadow to the outer edges of her eyelids, as well as more mascara to her lashes. I also did more contouring and applied a deeper shade of lipstick than that used in her commercial shot. On top of this, I put another dollop of gloss in the center of the lower lip; I find that gloss spread over both lips is distracting because it reflects so many highlights.

Next, I swung her beautiful red hair to one side so that it cascaded down her shoulder. Ann wore a sequined jacket worn over a silk print blouse and a double-strand gold necklace and gold-hoop earrings. Together, they complete her glamorous image. Even the position of Ann's head enhances her sophisticated appearance.

For both of these headshots, my purpose was to make Ann look like she was performing in a cabaret or club. As such, I used a 650-watt flood in spotlight mode with a medium diffuser on her face rather than a scoop light, which provides a broader spread of illumination. I backlit her hair with two 150-watt spotlights and then added some bounce light from an aluminum reflector.

ANN McCORMACK

ANN McCORMACK

THE MATURE LEADING LADY

After finishing Christine Child's commercial and industrial shots, which she intended to use to get acting jobs and to serve as public-relations pictures for her work as director of a children's theater, I made a subtle glamour shot of her. She changed into a black-velvet dress embroidered with tiny pearls. Upon my seeing her, I had a creative urge. Christine's dress reminded me of those seen in Cecil Beaton photographs. I knew that I had the right dress to recapture this look, but at first I wasn't sure of what to do about the background. I certainly couldn't fly the two of us over to Windsor Castle, so I had to come up with something "royal" but in keeping with my budget.

Fortunately, I remembered that Beaton used draped backgrounds in many of his shots, too. I draped a white mosquito netting that I'd brought from my country house to my New York City studio behind Christine. This background provided just the right touch. And my subject's regal bearing augmented the feeling. This approach resulted in a successful commercial shot.

For Marilyn Heitman's commercial shot, she wore a simple plaid top and projected a great deal of charm. Here, I used a softly diffused key light, a soft backlight on her hair, a reflector for fill, and a gray background. Her dark-gray hair was styled back and away from her face; her bright eyes appear to be looking straight at the viewer. Neither her makeup nor her earrings detract from her sparkling personality. This portrait of a friendly, attractive woman is sure to enable Marilyn to continue doing both commercials and print advertisements.

Christine Child

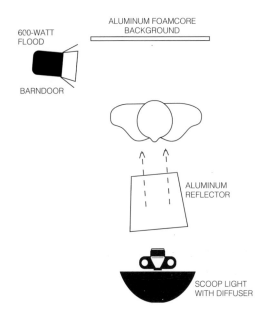

600-WATT FLOOD

BARNDOOR

ALUMINUM FOAMCORE BACKGROUND

ALUMINUM REFLECTOR

SCOOP LIGHT WITH DIFFUSER

Marilyn Heitman

THE VERSATILE ACTRESS

Singer/actress Susan Shamroy displays her winning smile in her commercial headshot, for which she wore a smart pleated-chiffon dress (right). Her exceptionally long eyelashes bring out her Elizabeth Taylor-like eyes. And to help her relax and to make the entire session pleasurable, I played one of her tapes. When designing the lighting setup for this photograph, I decided to use soft highlighting in order to accent her curly hair.

Susan then turned on the allure for her glamour shot. Here, I'd planned to drape some gold-lamé fabric behind Susan in order to give this portrait a Hollywood feel. Makeup artist Krista Lorn intensified the makeup she'd done earlier for Susan's commercial shot. Krista applied more mascara to Susan's eyelashes and a touch more gloss to her client's lips. She also let my subject borrow a black sequined jacket, which Susan placed over her strapless dress. She can use this headshot, in which she looks quite sophisticated, for her singing appearances, as well as for soap operas and films if the director is looking for a stunning woman.

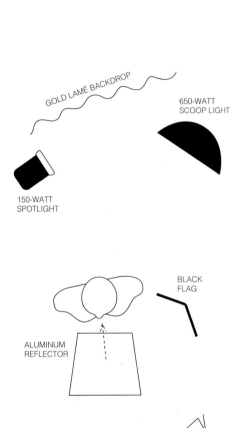

GOLD LAMÉ BACKDROP

650-WATT
SCOOP LIGHT

150-WATT
SPOTLIGHT

BLACK
FLAG

ALUMINUM
REFLECTOR

650-WATT
KEY LIGHT

Susan Shamroy

THE ELEGANT, UPSCALE LOOK

Older women are often asked to play classy ladies. These roles might include opera stars, Park Avenue types who shop all day long and have lunch at an expensive restaurant, and owners of cosmetic companies. Mature actresses, then, need a headshot that shows that they are ideally suited for such parts.

As Alice Spivak's commercial headshot indicates, this actress and acting teacher can easily play an elegant woman who lives on New York City's East Side. The drop earrings and beautiful textured blouse serve to reinforce this idea of sophistication. I used a minimal amount of makeup here: no strong eye shadow, a medium shade of lipstick, and some blush under her cheekbones. To provide my subject with flattering illumination, I positioned the main light directly at my client's face and a 150-watt light on her hair to bring out its highlights. I kept the background on the light side to contrast it with Alice's dark hair and flowered top. My final preparatory step was to aim a gently blowing fan at her hair.

Alice Spivak

A STAR IS BORN

Actress/Tony Award winner Debra Monk returns to my studio to have new headshots taken every year or two. For this commercial shot, she wore a polo shirt with the open collar turned up slightly. This is all the costuming that Debra needs in order to make a great impression because of her talent and engaging personality. Here, her short hair was brushed back a bit over the eyes so that they were readily visible. This successful photograph reveals Debra's vibrant, smiling presence and suggests that she is a true professional.

Paulette Attie is a cabaret singer with a sparkling stage personality. When she came to my studio requesting glamour headshots, I realized that this consummate performer would make a great impression through her photographs. I also knew that I would have only to suggest some different angles and head positions in order to capture the look and feeling we wanted to create. Here, I directed Paulette to tilt her head and used the main light as a spotlight, an effect you see in cabarets. I even added some glitzy starbursts in the background to enhance this alluring effect. For this glamour headshot, I intensified Paulette's makeup. The finishing touches are her dressy costume, complete with feather boa, and glittering earrings.

Debra Monk

Paulette Attie

LIGHTING TECHNIQUES

The lighting designs needed for mature leading ladies are basically identical to those used for subjects in other age ranges. The equipment, such as the key light, backlight, and fill light, is positioned much the same way. And making the images bright and airy for older women is just as important as it is for younger female clients.

When photographing nightclub/cabaret singer Lori G., I wanted to create a spotlight effect for her commercial headshot because she is such a wonderful performer. Here, she wore a simple white, open-collared blouse and a huge smile. Her ability to project her exuberant personality is exceptional. To illuminate Lori effectively, I aimed my 650-watt Lowell lamp on her face to make her look as if she is in a follow spot on a stage. A reflector tilted under her chin provided fill, and a 650-watt scoop backlit her curly blonde hair.

Constance Barron is another electrifying performer. Because of her sparkling personality, which almost makes her black-and-white photographs seem to be in color, she is quite busy doing musical-theater,

industrial, and commercial work, as well as voiceovers. For this commercial headshot, she selected a simple cream-colored, scoop-neck, linen blouse. Her hair was brushed in a soft, full style that framed her attractive face. Constance knows her makeup requirements very well. She creates a very natural look by applying a base that is slightly tanner than her light skin tone, and a deep-pink blush just under her cheekbones. Her shade of lipstick is also deep pink, and she forgoes dark lip liner. She uses dark-brown mascara but very little eyeliner on her lower lids.

To show Constance off to her best advantage, I surrounded her with flattering illumination, particularly her face. As a result, she seems to glow in this picture. To achieve this look, I aimed a lamp at her face at a 45-degree angle. Next, I added a generous amount of fill light from below her chin, which I softened with some diffusion. Hollywood cinematographers discovered this effective lighting technique years ago, and it is still utilized today. Think "light and bright." I intensely dislike photographs of actresses that appear grayish and overly shadowed. Printing Constance's 8 x 10 headshot for a slightly high-key look enhanced the result of this lighting design.

Lori G

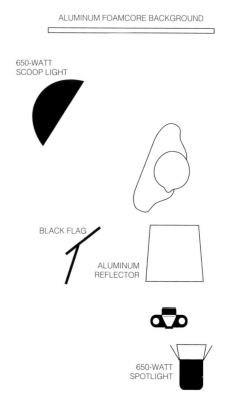

ALUMINUM FOAMCORE BACKGROUND

650-WATT
SCOOP LIGHT

BLACK FLAG

ALUMINUM
REFLECTOR

650-WATT
SPOTLIGHT

Constance Barron

CHAPTER NINE

PHOTOGRAPHING OLDER MEN

When men reach the age of 40, their faces become quite interesting, which, in turn, makes your work as a headshot photographer even more interesting. Men in this age group have a great sense of self, and this enables you to capture the laid-back, assured look that you want in a professional headshot. These subjects don't require any more makeup than they did when they were younger because they're getting acting work for who they are at this point in their lives. When asked about their age or appearance, older men often comment, "I've earned these lines." Wardrobe choices for these clients, like those for other subjects, should be simple, not distracting. The men's hair should ideally be medium length, and their attitude should be straightforward and honest.

Although many actors automatically deduct 10 years when asked about their age, this isn't necessary. Some people look older than they are, while others look younger than their years. Furthermore, when searching for a particular type of performer, most casting personnel try to find someone in the right age range. This usually covers a five-year span that affords an actor some leeway.

Don Uehling's photograph is a perfect example of a mature leading man's headshot. In this legit shot, he comes across as suave and sophisticated; this air brings to mind Sean Connery in the James Bond films and Clint Eastwood in the Dirty Harry films. Here, Don wore a white scoop-neck sweater over a white turtleneck. As is customary with male subjects, his hairstyle and makeup aren't elaborate. I simply used a subtle medium base first and then applied a terra-cotta tan blush over the face. Next, I brushed Don's medium-length hair with a little hair spray and then backlit it without undue fanfare.

Don Uehling

WARDROBE RECOMMENDATIONS

Clothing choices for older leading men are basically the same as those for other subjects. For commercial headshots, denim shirts are fine for any age range, but leather and denim jackets are inappropriate for mature males. For legit shots, these subjects are better off sticking with casual tweed jackets, polo shirts, and pastel button-down shirts. Scoop-neck sweaters over light shirts are good choices, too. To round out the wardrobe selection, tell clients to bring one dark (black or navy) suit, as well as one gray suit to be on the safe side; dark suits can often look too severe.

Harry Geng's composite shows him sporting three similar yet distinct outfits. In his leading-man/industrial shot, he looks dapper and urbane (left). He wore a suit,

a striped tie, and a big watch. I wanted casting people to see that Harry has goods hands, so I instructed him to hold a cigarette. For his legit shot, Harry changed into a tweed jacket and an open-collared oxford shirt (top right). The resulting image is casually elegant.

Harry's commercial shot reveals a big smile under his handsome mustache (bottom right). For this photograph, he chose an understated suit and tie and a white shirt. The overall impression this composite makes is that of a chief executive officer who is just as comfortable on Park Avenue as he is at the America's Cup yacht races. For diversity among these headshots, I directed Harry to angle his head a bit for some of the pictures and to hold his head straight for others.

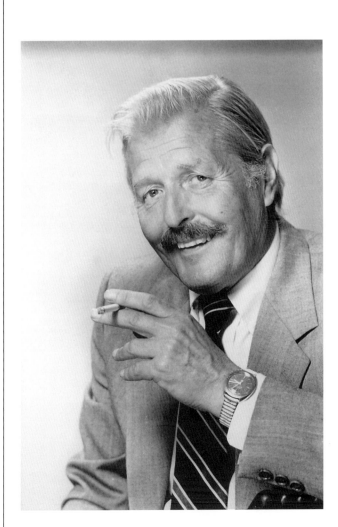

Harry Geng

CAPTURING A PERSONA

As a headshot photographer, you must work hard in order to accurately depict individual aspects of the talent who come to you for pictures. Although making wardrobe choices with your subjects can provide you with a sense of who they are, capturing the personality of each clients is a challenge. To achieve this goal, you must listen carefully to your subjects when they talk about their work, be interested in it, and make it part of your life at that particular moment in time, too!

When you work, you should try to make all of your subjects feel as if they are exceptional talents with a niche in the world of the performing artist. This is essential. Subjects reveal their personas through their facial characteristics and intellects, as well as by the way they want to present themselves to their public.

Director Leslie B. Cutler has a strong face and penetrating eyes that speak right to you. For this legit/publicity shot, Leslie wore a simple, white Egyptian-cotton shirt because he is an informal kind of man; however, this casual approach doesn't influence his always being in charge. Notice his hand's unusual resting position here, which sets this picture apart.

Ordinarily, most headshot backgrounds are pretty simple. But when planning a shooting session with Nick Fedyn, he and I agreed that the final composite images should resemble advertisements that have realistic-looking backgrounds. I also wanted to achieve scope in this composite by showing Nick in various guises. This idea evolved because I'd just finished painting several backgrounds. Nick and I then discussed wardrobe changes and props that would complement them, and I planned to use my standard lighting design (strong key light and background fill) because I knew that it would suit them best.

In one commercial shot, Nick donned construction-worker garb, complete with a hardhat and a red Pendleton shirt, and stood in front of a sky backdrop (top left). He then changed into a chef's outfit for another commercial headshot; looming behind him is the Roman Coliseum, which establishes an Italian-restaurant theme (top right). For an unusual legit shot, Nick donned a doctor's white coat (bottom left). Together with the prop eyeglasses and stethoscope, the folding-screen panel authenticates this image. For Nick's industrial shot, he wore a blue serge suit and a conservative striped tie, pretending to be a senator from the Midwest (bottom right). He looks quite self-assured as he stands in front of a backdrop showing the Capitol steps. Obviously, Nick and I had a great deal of fun during this shooting session.

LESLIE B. CUTLER

NICK FEDYN

THE MATURE LEADING MAN

Headshot photographers must be sensitive to facial changes in older male performers. Photographers must help actors accept the fact that the signs of aging visible in their faces are merely proof that they've developed character. Portrait photographers need to prepare clients for the inevitable aging they'll experience with humor, tact, and diplomacy.

Don Owen's formal and informal headshots reveal a mature leading man with a face with character lines, but which is nonetheless quite appealing. These two photographs give you a clear idea of the different looks you can achieve with a client. For his leading-man shot, Don wore a snappy bow tie (below). I added the yellow-silk pocket handkerchief for extra dash. Next, he switched into a cotton work shirt to create a casual sports-oriented look (right).

I used the same lighting setup for both of Don's headshots. The key light was a 650-watt scoop; this strong, round light threw a large area of somewhat softened illumination that was focused enough to concentrate on the subject's face and torso. I then placed an aluminum reflector on a stand just below Don's face. This fill, or bounce, light eliminated the facial shadows that the key light caused, as well as added extra sparkle to the subject's eyes.

DON OWEN

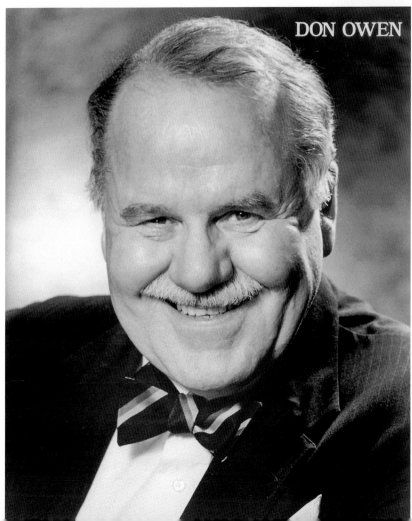

DON OWEN

CHARACTER ACTORS

These actors have such strong faces that they make terrific foils for the often atypical leading men they play opposite. The professional careers of character actors often last much longer than those of the leads for a few reasons. First, character actors are open to a much wider variety of roles than leading men are, so they frequently work more as a result. And unlike stars who are continually concerned about how long their looks will last, character actors don't have to give this potential problem much thought.

What makes character actors so popular with headshot photographers, however, is that they are much easier to photograph than other types of actors. Character actors' special facial features work so well them for that shooting a great picture of these clients is simple. You have only to get them to relax and be themselves—and, of course, to relate to the camera.

For Sean Griffin's legit headshot, he wore a white, open-collared shirt underneath a dark V-neck sweater. This basic wardrobe combination provided the perfect unobtrusive wardrobe this character actor needed for this portrait. Rather than noticing Sean's clothes, agents and managers will pay attention to his unusual face. His eyebrows, which slope down over his eyes, and the slightly upturned corners of his mouth combine to make him appear bemused. This expression reveals Sean's versatility as an actor who can look any way he is directed to.

Returning to my studio for updated headshots, character actor Bill Galarno told me that he wanted a different look. During his visit, he and I discussed the wardrobe requirements for industrial headshots. This type of picture is appropriate for casting calls for, among other venues, soap operas. An agent might be looking for an older man with a mustache and beard to play a doctor, pharmacist, or accountant. A suit, a light-toned shirt, and a tie are de rigueur for industrial shots. Here, Bill wore a suit with a fine tweed, a white shirt, and a striped tie. The result: an effective Wall Street/Madison Avenue image, complete with the self-confident air and straightforward gaze that are necessary for an industrial headshot.

Sean Griffin

Bill Galarno

Ashley J. Laurence

A lively character actor with his own style, Ashley J. Laurence has worked with a number of great film directors, including Herbert Ross, Elia Kazan, and Franco Zefferelli. Ashley's engaging smile and friendly face dominate the wardrobe he selected for his commercial headshot. He wore an unusual combination, which consisted of a checked shirt, a tweed jacket, and a black silk tie.

THE CORPORATE LOOK

While I planned actor John Henry Cox's session with him, he made it emphatically clear that he wanted a power-broker image to market himself as a suitable candidate for both industrial and commercial work. John knew exactly what to wear in order to achieve this stern, "titan of industry" look. He'd planned every detail of his wardrobe, down to his striped shirt with a white collar, collar pin, and cuff links. The white-silk handkerchief that was placed in his jacket pocket proved to be both a perfect topper and the ideal design element to complete this graphic image.

Since I wanted to shoot up at my subject, I aimed a 600-watt spotlight at flood at John's face and used a reflector under his chin for fill. Next, I backlit him with a 150-watt light from behind his right shoulder. I selected a dark textured background to provide a strong base for this striking shot; I didn't hit the backdrop with any light.

TEXTURED BACKDROP

150-WATT
SPOTLIGHT

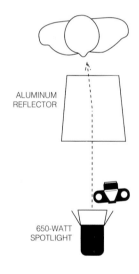

ALUMINUM
REFLECTOR

650-WATT
SPOTLIGHT

John Henry Cox

Naturally, when you photograph a real executive rather than an actor pretending to be one, you don't have to worry about wardrobe. These clients can simply select clothes that they ordinarily wear to work. I photographed Irving Goldman, a real-estate executive/philanthropist, in his New York City office. When I first got there, he was sitting behind his huge L-shaped desk; I sensed immediately that he was busy and distracted. But Irving relaxed when his energetic grandson arrived. In fact, playing with the little boy in and around the desk put everyone involved with the shoot at ease. I simply pointed my 650-watt Lowell spotlight at my subject and snapped away, being sure to compensate for the backlighting from the window. My subject comes across as a high-powered but friendly executive in this headshot.

Photographing Wall Street executive Philip Wong proved to be challenging in a different way. I faced serious time constraints in this situation because of Philip's hectic schedule. As a matter of fact, I had only enough time to select an interesting corner of the meeting room and then to get to work. I quickly decided to shoot against the glass bricks in one part of the room. I then asked my subject in a chair at the table, and put some paper down on the table to make this scene seem more real. Next, I directed Philip to hold his pen, and gave him my usual advice about relaxing and being friendly toward the camera.

For this shot, I'd packed my trusty 650-watt Lowell spotlight and a fold-up aluminum reflector. I aimed this diffused spotlight at Philip at a 45-degree angle at the other end of the small boardroom table. This provided bounced light on his face. Next, I placed the aluminum fabric on the table just in front of my client's hands but out of the lower end of the picture framing.

Keep in mind that whenever you make executive portraits, you confront the business tensions that come with the territory; this is especially true when you shoot in your clients' office. To help the session run smoothly, you might want to make a list of the pieces of equipment you need to bring to the location; you don't want to arrive without a much-needed extension cord, flash attachment, or umbrella, for example. It is also a good idea to arrive fresh and a little early if possible. Then try to remain relaxed yourself, and assure your subjects that you won't try to take up too much of their time. Executives are invariably in a hurry, so put them at ease immediately by letting them know that you know what you're doing. Be prepared to adjust to their pace, too. Most important, however, is getting them to feel comfortable in front of the camera. Finally, act like the consummate professional photographer you are.

IRVING GOLDMAN

Philip Wong

LIGHTING TECHNIQUES

James Cole

James Cole, who has appeared on various television shows and in many commercials, is as forceful a subject as any headshot photographer could ask for. He has also done a great deal of print work, so his connection with the camera is especially acute and effective. His ability to relate to the camera is self-evident in these three headshots.

Because James didn't have an outdoor shot, I decided to take him on location for his commercial shot (left). Here, he wore an open-collared denim shirt, as well as his very professional but very real smile. Photographing my subject on a porch, I needed only available light to capture his true personality.

For James's leading-man picture, which I shot indoors, he decided to go with a very formal approach (below); he wore his evening best, a tuxedo, and looked smashing. I opted for my customary strong key-light/fill-light combination. Next, I backlit his hair just enough to make it read handsome white and then kept the background dark gray to offset it.

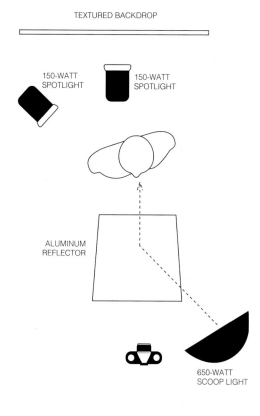

TEXTURED BACKDROP

150-WATT SPOTLIGHT

150-WATT SPOTLIGHT

ALUMINUM REFLECTOR

650-WATT SCOOP LIGHT

Finally, for James's industrial shot, he changed into a dark-blue serge suit, a tailored shirt, and a patterned silk tie (above). Together, these wardrobe pieces made him seem as if he belonged in the boardroom of a Fortune 500 company. The lighting setup consisted of a 650-watt main light angled at his face from a high position; an aluminum reflector providing fill light; and two 150-watt soft spotlights, one aimed at the background, and one aimed at James's back.

CHAPTER TEN

AFTER YOU SHOOT

Many clients have only a vague understanding of what happens after a session. They remember that during the initial interview you told them that you would take two or three rolls of film on the day of the shoot. The pictures were shot; the session is over. Now what? What do you do with the film?

You have two options. You can develop and contact print the rolls of film yourself or you can have them processed at a professional lab. I've always used a professional lab. I've gotten excellent results from several labs in New York City, including J. Beninati Custom Laboratories, Dan Demetriad Professional Photographic Services, and Modernage Custom Color Labs. I've done a great deal of work with Joe Beninati during the last five years, and I've been lucky to have had the same printer, Andy, for much of that time. Andy knows my style and gives me prints exactly the way I want them. After the film is developed and printed, you determine with your client which shots to enlarge and to include in the all-important composite.

Composites vary according to your subjects' needs and desires. Some clients want to use only one headshot, while others may decide to show a few different looks. Some subjects want to provide only their name, and others want to provide more personal information. This is an individual preference.

Anna Chamblée looks chic in all of her pictures. This is the way she comes across when you meet her, and it is the image that she wanted to present in her composite. She decided to use three photographs. In her two commercial headshots, she is smiling, and her head positions differ. She also included a full-length shot in order to make her composite suitable for modeling work. This photograph shows off Anna's lithe figure, her lovely way of moving, and her hands. A few rays of sunlight came in through the studio window and intruded on my lighting design, but I left them in because I felt that they added a splash of visual interest to my subject's long black gown.

Because Anna seeks out modeling jobs, she thought that listing her vital statistics on her composite was important. She also indicated that she has excellent hands and legs; this is noteworthy because models can often make $250 an hour simply with their hands.

ANNA CHAMBLÉE

DRESS: 6
HEIGHT: 5'4"
BUST: 34A
WAIST: 26
SHOE: 7½M

HIPS: 36
HAIR: DK. BROWN
EYES: DK BROWN
GLOVE: 7
EXCELLENT HANDS & LEGS

CHECKING CONTACT SHEETS

After shooting three rolls of film on average and then reassuring your clients that the entire shoot went well, you'll make an appointment with them to look at the resulting contact sheets (or proofs) at another specified time and/or place. I usually meet my clients at the Beninati Lab in midtown Manhattan one or two days after the session. I reassuringly tell my subjects that I am as anxious to see the shots as they are. Although I've heard that some photographers keep their clients waiting one or two weeks before showing them the contact sheets, I think that this is a bad business practice.

If you've shot 35mm film, each contact sheet will contain approximately 36 separate frames on it, as you can see on Matt Kowalski's contact sheet. If you've shot 2¼ film, however, each contact sheet will have only 12 shots on it. Naturally, since the 2¼ format is bigger than the 35mm format, checking the pictures is easier; however, I don't like the larger format because of its inherent framing and cropping problems. Furthermore, I know that by my using the new, better-quality 105mm portrait lenses on my favorite 35mm Nikon camera, the resulting images will be sharp enough for 8 x 10 enlargements.

When you study the contact sheets for the first time, make sure that they are sharp and carefully laid out, and have enough contrast for easy viewing. Check for blurry and fogged images. Don't accept sheets that have been printed in a sloppy manner.

The next step in the headshot process is to examine the 35mm frames together with your clients. To do this properly, you need a loupe, which is a magnifying glass that enables you to see details. I prefer battery-powered loupes because they allow for better pinpointed illumination than manual loupes do. While I go over the contact sheets with clients, I tell them that I'll work with them from beginning to end during the headshot process; I even offer to help them select the style of lettering they want for their name imprint on the 8 x 10 glossy.

As my subjects and I choose our favorite six or seven shots from each series or changes of clothes, I mark those frames with a red grease pencil. Look first for personality projection, a relaxed attitude, good eye contact with the camera, and appropriate wardrobe. Select the frames that pop out at you.

Then, unless my clients have a tight deadline, I ordinarily recommend that they take the contact sheets home and look at the images at their leisure. Most subjects have signed with an agent or manager who, in turn, will want to go over the contact sheets with them. After a day or two, the clients bring the sheets back, and we make our final selections. The goal is to choose the three best images. These shots are then blown up as promised in the headshot package (additional enlargements are $20 each).

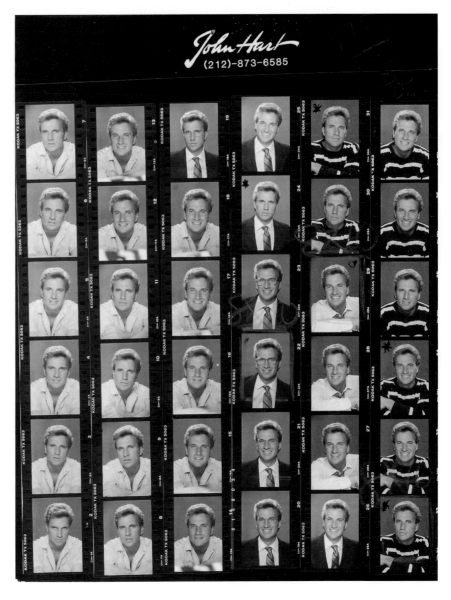

THE REPRODUCTION PROCESS

After my subjects and I select the three best shots, I have the images printed. Next, I go over the enlargements with the clients once again to see if the pictures require any retouching. If the lighting, makeup, and hair were done carefully, this should be minimal. But the 8 x 10 glossies aren't necessarily complete yet. Many agents and managers who work with children want their own logo to appear under the clients' photograph. This trademark identifies who represents the young talent and enables interested parties to get in touch with the rep quickly if there is a booking. These logos are kept on file at labs so that they can easily be imprinted on enlargements along with the subject's name. If new talent don't have an agent yet, printing just their own name is fine. Sometimes, the telephone number of a contact, such as an agent, is placed behind or under the subject's name. As a result, telephone calls are screened before parents hear them.

When the final headshot images are finished, clients often ask how to get reproductions made. I explain that in order to do this, a custom lab or reproduction house needs to use the enlargement, not the original negatives. The printer takes the 8 x 10 glossy and rephotographs it to get a second-generation 8 x 10 copy negative. It is from this copy negative that the printer will make the number of reproductions the subject requests; this figure might be anywhere from 50 to 100. Prices for reproductions vary, but they usually cost about $65 for 100. Your clients also pay for and keep the copy negative. Then when they need to have more reproductions made, they simply bring it back to the lab and order more.

Once the reproduction process is complete, which takes an average of five business days, the reproduced headshots are ready. Clients can then either give them to their agent to submit them to casting directors, or if they're looking for an agent or manager, they can mail them out to prospects in 9 x 11 envelopes. The pictures should be protected by cardboard and accompanied perhaps by a short cover letter. Before sending out their headshots, some clients attach a simple resumé to the back that lists such personal data as their telephone number, age, hair and eye colors, height, weight, and clothes size. They usually describe any theatrical, film, or commercial experience and mention any unions that they belong to. In addition, subjects often include their interest in sports, as well as talents, such as singing, dancing, or playing the piano.

For Philip Mauro's commercial headshot, I directed him to look over his shoulder at the camera and to flash a big smile. He cooperated, and the result is a great portrait of a vibrant nine-year-old. On the back of this headshot is Philip's resumé, which indicates that he has brown hair and eyes, is 48 inches tall, and weighs 53 pounds. It also lists the print work he has done for G. Fox, J. C. Penney, and Caldor stores, the professional training he received at "The Soap Set," and his football, swimming, and karate skills.

I feel that it is important to guide clients throughout the entire reproduction process because it can seem a bit mysterious to those just starting out in the entertainment business. Like the picture-taking, this will put your subjects at ease and make them more willing to work with you if they know that you'll be there for them every step of the way.

Phillip
Mauro

Ralph & Lisa Mauro
10 Leigh Drive
East Haven, CT 06512
TEL: (203) 469-5508
(203) 467-3681

PHILLIP MAURO

AGE RANGE:	**9 YEARS**
HAIR:	**BROWN**
EYES:	**BROWN**
HEIGHT:	**48 INCHES**
WEIGHT:	**53 POUNDS**
SIZE:	**10–12**
SHOE SIZE:	**4–5**

COMMERCIALS:	*List upon request*
PRINT:	*G. FOX*
	J. C. PENNEY
	CALDOR'S
TRAINING:	*THE SOAP SET*
SKILLS:	*Dancing (freestyle), singing, football, nature walking, swimming, bicycle riding, karate*

RETOUCHING

When some clients see their three 8 × 10 enlargements for the first time, they're amazed that they've acquired so many lines in their face. You want to reply that they've earned each and every one of them and these signs of age are barely discernible. But, instead, you tell them the truth—that everyone needs a little touching up.

You should also point out to your clients that unlike color images, black-and-white photographs don't lessen complexion flaws. In fact, these shots often exaggerate skin problems. And although you and your makeup artist take great care with lighting and makeup to hide facial aberrations, you can't always completely camouflage some features, such as an acne scar or a deep line. It can also help to define and accentuate makeup. Simply remember, and remind your clients, that you are a photographer, not a plastic surgeon. Furthermore, you are in the business of making people look like themselves at their best, not other people.

To understand the potential benefits of skillful retouching, which is done before reproductions are run off, take a look at Joey Templeton's portraits. Hot off the drying drum, her original 8 × 10 enlargement shows no sign of being altered (left). I then decided to do a little retouching, as you can see in her final reproduction (right). With my trusty Spotone No. 3, a neutral black liquid that matches most printing-paper emulsions, and a Robert Simmons No. 1/61-R very-fine sable-hair brush, I proceeded to go over Joey's makeup. She has fabulous eyelashes, so all I had to do was define them a bit for stronger reproduction. I then added a bit more contouring to her cheekbones and reduced the highlights on her hair, especially those near her left shoulder.

Next, I noticed that the shadow under her left eye was a bit darker than the one on her right. To fix this, I took my double-edged Gillette razor blade, which was carefully cut in two and the top edge covered with masking tape. I carefully etched away the grain and lightened the darkness. Don't be concerned if the blade goes into the top layer of emulsion; you can wash the whiteness that is exposed with Spotone. I use exactly the same process to work on lines and blemishes. When you take a close look at Joey's final shot, you can tell where I did the strengthening, lightening, and shading that gives the photograph punch and dimension.

I prefer to do my own retouching and usually charge $10 to $20 for each print depending on the amount of work involved. If you feel some resistance to this, just remember that no photograph gets into any publication without some retouching. Of course, some people go to extremes to improve a subject's appearance in a picture. For example, the airbrushing technique always verges on being too artificial looking because it eliminates skin texture too much. Computer-assisted manipulation can also seem rather contrived, and it takes an expert to accomplish. Furthermore, both of these alteration procedures are quite expensive; as such, they are out of the realm of possibility of becoming routine.

Be aware that when asked about retouching clients' headshots, some agents reply, "I don't want any retouching. I want them to look the way they do when I see them in the office." Agents want basic realism in a photograph. As a result, they consider airbrushing completely out of the question. This attitude is somewhat unrealistic because studio lighting is much more intense than office lighting.

THE COMPOSITE

Clients have two choices when it comes to composites. Glossy composites printed on paper are actually photographic prints, and are relatively inexpensive. This type of composite is fine for new talent interested in doing both acting and modeling. The other option is to have litho composites made. Most models and modeling agencies prefer this kind of composite because it has two sides. These composites must be done, incidentally, at a litho printer who specializes in doing two-, three-, and four-page printed composites. Not surprisingly, litho composites are more expensive initially than glossy composites, but clients get several hundred more of them.

To give a composite a strong graphic design, I tell my clients to consider putting a black border around their headshots. This separates the photograph from the white background and helps it to stand out. I also warn them to make sure that the white background order isn't so wide that it detracts from the pictures. Remember, the headshots are what casting directors, agents, and managers should notice first, not the white space surrounding the photographs.

As your subjects will learn, many different commercial labs do composites—with varying prices and quality. Tell your subjects to shop around carefully. If clients use a lab that I patronize, I offer to help them design the layout of the composite. However, if clients go to another lab, I simply give them their enlargements and make some recommendations regarding picture placement.

Keith Perkins's four-headshot composite is all that it should be. His attention-grabbing closeup commercial photograph is in the upper right-hand corner, which is the spot a viewer's eye is drawn to first. The remaining pictures show Keith in various poses and outfits. He looks like a busy executive in the two industrial shots (top left, bottom right), and a relaxed "nice guy" in his legit shot (bottom left). The overall impression this composite makes is that Keith is a versatile actor.

Keith Perkins

POSTCARDS

Another important part of the reproduction process involves the creation of postcards. These provide one of the most effective ways for aspiring performers to stay in touch with casting directors and agents. Actors have to remain in frequent contact with and keep their faces in front of the powers that be; they can't sit around waiting for the telephone to ring with a fabulous job offer. This is self-defeating and delusional. They have to let casting people know that they are available for work. The postcard has taken the place of the telephone call, during which an actor would ask an agent either "What's happening?" or "Anything for me today?" Because of the increase in competition and the hundreds of performers agents handle today, they don't have time to field calls from perhaps hundreds of clients.

Once clients send out their 8 x 10 headshot with a resumé attached, receive a call expressing interest in them, and then interview or audition, they should follow up with postcard mailouts. These smaller versions of the actors' headshot serve to remind agents and casting directors of their very recent meeting.

Because postcard formats available from your local reproduction house vary so much, deciding which one is right for a particular client can be difficult. The standard 4 x 6 double-weight postcard can contain a single headshot, as Neil Butterfield's mailout shows. Note, too, that Neil's picture is surrounded by a white border, but the picture can also bleed all the way to the edge of the card across three sides. Another choice is to use two headshots to reveal different sides of their personality, thereby giving them an advantage. Like most people who work with children, Dana Margiotta's agent decided that this approach would work better for his young client. Her postcard shows this dynamo's happy and serious sides.

Your clients' next step is to determine what to have printed on the postcard. Bill and Neil decided to include only their own names and telephone numbers. But as you can see on Dana's postcard, her manager's name and number also appear; this makes for easy identification.

Still another option is to go with a bigger format and have 5 x 7 postcards made up. While these do attract more attention than small postcards, they are also more expensive and can require additional postage. Whether you choose a small or large format, all postcards are shot down to size from the subjects' original 8 x 10 retouched prints. Perhaps most important, postcards go a long way in promoting the air of professionalism that makes the agents, casting directors, and managers take notice of your acting clients.

While agents and/or managers are the final arbiters of the way their talent pool will be presented, the photographer's own good taste and advice are essential. Professional headshot photographers are hired because they have a reputation for being the best at what they do: photographing great headshots. Managers, agents, and parents respect this talent and, consequently, respect the input that the photographers offer. They are the experts, and thanks to their years of experience know what works best. Creating compelling headshots is, after all, a team effort from beginning to end.

Neil Butterfield
(212) 417-9411

Personal Management
ESTELLE & ALPHONSO, INC.
212-702-0410

Dana Margiotta

HELPING ACTORS GET STARTED

You've given your clients the very best headshots in town. Now they need to do something with their portraits. You can help clients get on their road to success and stardom. Although having a relative who just happens to be one of the top agents at William Morris would be ideal, actors can take advantage of dozens of professional sources available to them. You can advise them as to where to look and what to do to break into the entertainment business.

WHERE TO MAIL HEADSHOTS

Although many of the people you photograph may already be working actors signed by agents, a large number are coming to you for their very first headshots. As a result, you shouldn't be surprised if they ask you if you know any agents or managers. Whenever I can, I recommend that these clients contact certain agents and managers who I know are always looking for new talent.

However, most agents and casting firms are too busy for blind contacts. Because of this, I ordinarily suggest to actors that they follow the time-tested method of mailing out their headshots in an envelope to the many agents listed in such publications as the *Ross Report, NYC*, and *The Madison Avenue Handbook*. Aspiring performers can buy these agency lists, as well as the names and addresses of advertising-agency and soap-opera casting people at various bookstores, including The Drama Book Shop and Applause Theatre Books in New York City. Another excellent source for neophyte actors is Mari Lynn Henry's *The Working Actor*. This is chock full of information about the ins and outs of show business: where to go, who to see, and how to be a professional while undergoing the traumatic experience of starting out in a very competitive field.

Incidentally, if novice actors want to earn some extra money by modeling for either fashion or commercial print work, I recommend Models Mart Ltd. in New York City. This store sells lists of modeling agencies, appointment books, and portfolios for photographs. Aspiring actors can also utilize most of the agency lists found at this store.

ACTING SCHOOLS

Many actors simply want to get started immediately and make quick money by doing television commercials. Clients who want to pursue this avenue have a large number of training schools to choose from. Many of these establishments' advertisements virtually guarantee work after individuals complete the required courses. Tell these clients that they can find an ample list of schools offering commercial-acting courses in *Backstage*, a weekly publication always available on newsstands. Although it can take most of a year for actors to get their feet wet, studying commercial-acting techniques certainly can't hurt. Your clients might also want to read Joan See's book, *Acting in Commercials: A Guide to Auditioning and Performing on Camera*.

Fledgling actors can sign up to take serious acting classes at numerous establishments in New York City, including AIA, the American Academy of Dramatic Arts, the Actor's Studio, HB Studios, the Maria Greco School, Take Two, and Three of Us. An added bonus: beginners will learn fast enough from other actors what is going on in town casting-wise.

All actors audit classes at these drama schools in order to determine if this particular approach is the type of experience they're looking for. Everyone has different ambitions when starting a career in the entertainment field, so it is absolutely critical to get started on the right path initially. Some newcomers want to perform as singers and dancers in musical comedies; others might want a strictly legit theatrical, television, or film career; and still others are hoping to make a fortune doing on-camera commercials or off-camera voice-overs. As you plan a shoot with performers, and later when you photograph them, listen carefully to their individual dreams and goals, and steer them in the right direction. Although this is tangential to your primary responsibility as a headshot photographer, it can only help you in the long run in terms of flattering word-of-mouth comments circulating within the acting community, which in turn may lead to new clients and repeat work.

CASTING CALL

Besides published books and advice from acting coaches and other actors, novice actors can look into professional newspapers that are published weekly on both the East and West Coasts for timely, current information about casting calls. These newsstand notices can range all the way from the casting needs of a New York University Film School student who is seeking actors for a project, to a high-profile director like Martin Scorsese who is looking for just the right types for his new film idea.

Publications that list casting calls include *Backstage*, a New York City-based weekly that keeps actors informed of the latest opportunities around the globe. Some of the columns in this newspaper are: Casting, Dance Diary, Reviews (of current Broadway and Off-Broadway productions), Regional Roundup (of out-of-town casting calls) Mid-Coast Cues, West Coast Stages, and London Calling. *Backstage* also contains editorials that discuss matters that are important to entertainers, such as show-business trends, hot topics, and actors' union news. A recent front-page article was entitled, "Getting Your Career Off to a Good Start." Obviously, this newspaper is invaluable to all aspiring actors.

New York Casting is another must-read newspaper for actors. Its masthead proclaims that it is "The Largest List of Casting Opportunities in the United States! Regularly running columns listed in the table of contents are: Answering Services; Bookstores; Instruction Classes; Coaches for Music, Speech, Voice; and Headshot Photographers. Actors will also find listings of plastic-surgery clinics.

Actors on the West Coast should get a copy of the very popular *Drama-Logue*, the bible for performers working in or near Los Angeles. In addition to film and commercial casting notices, this newspaper contains such bylines as Theatre Beat, as well as many celebrity-oriented interviews.

As a headshot photographer who is genuinely interested in your clients, you might want to consider keeping current copies of these various newspapers in your studio. This will give you a jumping-off place during the initial interview. It will also serve to reassure aspiring actors and other performers that the entertainment industry is thriving and is always looking for a new face—possibly theirs, thanks to the great headshots you are about to shoot for them.

INDEX